KINGDOM
REVOLUTION

KINGDOM REVOLUTION

BRINGING
CHANGE
TO YOUR LIFE
AND
BEYOND

JOSEPH MATTERA

DESTINY IMAGE® PUBLISHERS, INC.

P.O. Box 310, Shippensburg, PA 17257-0310

"Speaking to the Purposes of God for This Generation and for the Generations to Come."

This book and all other Destiny Image, Revival Press, MercyPlace, Fresh Bread, Destiny Image Fiction, and Treasure House books are available at Christian bookstores and distributors worldwide.

For a U.S. bookstore nearest you, call 1-800-722-6774.

For more information on foreign distributors, call 717-532-3040.

Reach us on the Internet: www.destinyimage.com.

ISBN 10: 0-7684-3099-2

ISBN 13: 978-0-7684-3099-8

For Worldwide Distribution, Printed in the U.S.A.

1 2 3 4 5 6 7 8 9 10 11 / 13 12 11 10 09

DEDICATION

I dedicate this book to the next generation of reformers who desire to see the Lordship of Christ bring transformation to all people and every nation.

ACKNOWLEDGMENTS

I want to acknowledge the following people who greatly aided me and made this book possible: Philip Sofia, my personal assistant; Vanessa Chandler, whose personal touch, creativity, and expert editing helped me know where to add anecdotal material to enhance the work; Pam McLaughlin, who edited and helped make my original work into two manuscripts; Dr. Larry Keefauver, who put the finishing touches on the book and gave me wise counsel; and the many friends and leaders who reviewed the manuscript and greatly encouraged me to persevere in the publishing process.

ENDORSEMENTS

Over the past few years, the Body of Christ has been blessed by a number of books on different aspects of "transformation" or "dominion" or "reformation," all pointing toward seeing God's Kingdom manifested here on earth. In *Kingdom Revolution,* Joseph Mattera, more than any of the rest, has skillfully pulled together all the threads into the most profound textbook on Kingdom theology currently available. If you are enlisting in the army of God, you definitely need this book!

C. Peter Wagner
Author, *Dominion!*

Dr. Mattera will teach and equip you in this significant book to understand covenant, develop a Kingdom mindset, and move from a paradigm of poverty into prosperity through impacting your culture and changing your world. Read this book and then step into a Christian perspective that will empower you to turn your world upside down!

Dr. Larry Keefauver

Churches and families across the nation are drastically losing the hearts of young people. Now, more than ever before, we are in need of a revolution. Joseph Mattera speaks directly and passionately on how we can all regain the Kingdom principles to transform lives outside of the church walls and bring Christ's life-giving message to the world.

Ron Luce
President and Founder, Teen Mania Ministries

In First Chronicles 12:32, the sons of Issachar had *"under-standing of the times, to know what Israel ought to do."* Pastor Joe Mattera is a contemporary "son of Issachar" and a respected leader in the NYC region. He understands the times we live in and through this book will help Christians and churches become more relevant and influential in our world today.

Ron Lewis
Senior Pastor, MSNY, New York
Founder, Stop Child Trafficking Now (SCTNow.org)

In *Kingdom Revolution* Joseph Mattera offers absolutely revolutionary and incendiary principles with balance and clarity. This is a magnificent book for Christian leaders to get "unstuck" and moving in the theology of the Kingdom.

Bishop Bill Atwood
Anglican Church of Kenya
General Secretary of Ekklesia

Joseph Mattera's new book is full of practical and compelling insights on the Kingdom of God. I expect that it will dramatically expand the horizons of those who read it. Christian leaders who are hungry for more will find *Kingdom Revolution* to be a feast of great ideas.

Archbishop Gregory Venables
Iglesia Anglicana del Cono Sur

Dr. Joseph Mattera is an exceptional leader who blends his brilliant worldview with a passion to impact all types of people. Joe has had an incredible impact on people all over the world and has an important message for leaders of all generations and in all places. This is an important book for leaders everywhere. His 25 years as a friend and colleague in New York City have been a great personal gift to me.

Dr. Mac Pier
President, The NYC Leadership Center

In this book, we are confronted with the "next level" of Christianity: will we "hold on" or "take over"? While most of us concede that we will never become the Kingdom of God without Jesus' presence here, we cannot use that as an excuse to remove ourselves from the marketplace of ideas and impact. Paul stood at Athens and confronted the most powerful and intellectual worldview of the early world.

I have personal respect for Joseph Mattera and his precious family. They have been solid and faithful to the Body of Christ in the Northeast for many years. They are accountable to authority and highly respected for commitment to the local church as pastors. They are disciplers and missionaries to a culture far removed from many parts of America.

You are going to have to "digest" this one! It is packed full of fundamental, yet relevant, information on a Christian worldview. *Bon appetit!*

Larry Stockstill

Bishop Mattera is to be commended for his pastoral work. He offers the reader a wonderful discussion on the importance of bringing our Christian faith to a world so hungry for its life-sustaining sustenance.

Firmly rooted in the rich Christian tradition of Vatican II, Dr. Martin Luther King, Bishop Tutu, and countless local pastors ministering in our own neighborhoods, Bishop Mattera challenges all Christians to engage the modern world with passion, intelligence, and faith.

With compassion for a world that seems to have lost its capacity to hear God's Word, Bishop Mattera presents an intelligent and passionate work that invites all Christians to evangelize where they are and with the people they encounter on a daily basis.

Catholic Deacon Kevin McCormick
Co-host, "Religion on the Line," WABC-AM, NYC

This work blows the fog off today's Church. Bishop Mattera explains why the Christian community should stop circling the wagons and start aggressively influencing our society. It communicates with remarkable clarity the biblical vision for today's Church as part of God's greater Kingdom mandate. With a firm foundation set in the Old Testament, Bishop Mattera provides leaders in the Church today with a vision for a better tomorrow. I can't wait to get this book into the hands of my leaders and the pastors in my city. It will unite us and cause a revolution in the entire city. Let the revolution begin with us!

Gary Hartley
Senior Pastor, Christ Fellowship
Elizabeth, New Jersey

Kudos to Bishop Mattera for this presentation of a clear, cohesive, and pragmatic theology of the Kingdom. *Kingdom Revolution* is a much-needed primer to restore God-centric foundations of cosmological significance. It can, if acted upon, assist any local church or any believer in personal advancement of their expression of the Gospel of Christ in all of life. Application of these powerful and pragmatic truths will deliver believers from slumber and awaken the overlooked truth of John 3:16, *"God so loved the kosmos...."*

Walter Healy

Bishop Joseph Mattera provides commonsense guidance for all of us who strive to live purposeful lives. It is a must-read.

Martin J. Golden
New York State Senator

Apostle Joseph Mattera has the unique gift and ability to take the complex and make it understandable. New revelation will lead to an internal revolution in your soul. The Kingdom of God, if understood correctly, will change you and your world forever. Apostle Mattera's apostolic mantle is to reveal the Kingdom. Are you ready for the revolution?

Dr. Samuel R. Chand
www.samchand.com

Bishop Joseph Mattera's book captures the essence of the culture clash in American society. As America breaks from its Puritan roots, a sense of meaninglessness and apathy is the natural result. Bishop Mattera explains not only the roots of the cultural decline, but also the biblical answers to restore our culture. Christians are called to be the salt and the light of the world through living Christ-centered lives. I highly recommend this book to anyone desiring to be part of the solution instead of part of the problem.

Orrin Woodward
Co-author of *NY Times* bestseller,
Launching a Leadership Revolution

Much of today's Church is marginalized when it comes to affecting the world's culture, increasingly powerless in light of society's values and priorities. We need a cutting-edge, prophetic voice to awaken a vibrant counterculture through the Church. Joe Mattera is that voice. The world's system will only be challenged by a more powerful culture—that is the dynamic, all-encompassing Kingdom of God. Joe has thoroughly researched the Kingdom, preached it, and practiced it. This book will empower you to be one of those voices. And the kairos moment is now—we cannot afford to wait.

Bob Philips
Pastor, Encourager Church
Houston, Texas

Bishop Mattera chronicles his rediscovery of the godly calling to transform culture and society as well as one's personal life. He calls upon each person to become responsible representatives for God in the cultural and civic arenas, and he provides a clear and practical theological foundation. This is the Bishop's best book so far!

Tony Carnes
President, Values Research Institute

Dr. Joseph Mattera delivers a digestible, relevant dose of apologetics in the vein of C.S. Lewis and G.K. Chesterton. He challenges us to get "outside the walls of church"—that it is the responsibility for Christians to redeem not only the Church but *all* facets of society—"to steward the earth as salt and light." Making the case for a holistic life and healed world, Joseph expounds that there is no "sacred vs. secular"—in the richness of pre-enlightenment teaching—it's all God! He then ties apologetics to the importance for us to understand multiple worldviews in order to teach *and live* a personal and societal awakening of the truth, beauty, and hope for the world—now and for eternity—which only a faith in Jesus Christ can deliver. Francis Schaeffer is clapping his hands for this new work by Dr. Mattera.

Linda Lindquist, Bishop
President, Courageous Thinking Inc.

Joseph Mattera has written a *tour de force!* He reveals that the Great Commission is the great *Cultural* Commission and discusses the challenges Christians have walking the tight rope of *being in the world, but not of the world*. This book is a must-read for all who believe *Thy kingdom shall come!*

Dr. John P. Kelly
CEO, International Christian Wealth Builders Foundation
Founder/President, Leadership
Education for Apostolic Development
Founder/Ambassador, International Coalition of Apostles

CONTENTS

FOREWORD

I first met Dr. Joseph Mattera in early 2005. We collaborated to bring hundreds of pastors together from around the New York City area to discuss a moral agenda that a national organization I led was spearheading. To my great delight, the group of leaders was unusually diverse. Black, white, Hispanic, and Asian leaders of regional consequence came together under the banner of the Kingdom of God. In addition, megachurch pastors sat with storefront church leaders to reason, relate, and respond to the unique needs of America's financial capital (New York City). I was immediately impressed with Joe Mattera's compassion, intellect, and grassroots organizational savvy.

Who is this man? I remember thinking to myself. The answer that came to mind was very clear. Dr. Mattera is a David for our generation. He has been raised up, beginning as shepherd of God's flock. On the battlefield of cultural valor, he has dared to challenge the Goliaths of our generation. Like David, he has been effective, using the proven weapons of his youth. Dr. Mattera is a spiritual general who has mastered the art of integrating genuine secular influence with the Lord's unique agenda for his city of origin. This book marks the beginning steps in his journey to take his message and methods to the entire nation and the world.

Over the years, I have found that Christian leaders typically fall into one of two categories—thinkers or doers. The thinkers often get hung up on elaborate teachings with very little practical application. They delight in developing theological definitions and convoluted paradigms for our behavior. Unfortunately, many Christians egg on these theorists because they have itching ears—desiring to hear the next exciting revelation from their "superstar" teachers.

On the other hand, I have met many activist leaders. These folks want to make a difference in practical ways in their cities. They are passionate and engaged. Unfortunately, activists often fall prey to discouragement and bitterness because of unrealistic expectations. In addition, because of their sense of urgency and their insistence on getting things done by any means necessary, they sometimes violate scriptural principles and fail to be good witnesses of the Kingdom of God.

Dr. Mattera is both a thinker and a doer. He is a purist and a pragmatist. He is a preacher and a politician. He is an ambassador of God and an agent of social change. Is he just one in million? I don't think so. He is the firstfruits of a new generation. He is a pioneer of a new kind of Christian activism.

The vision of this book is best explained by repeating the title of a secular book I have recently discovered: *Tribes: We Need You to Lead Us,* by Seth Godin. Dr. Mattera is making an appeal to each one of us to accept our calling to leadership. Your gifts may be different than his, but you are just as needed in this important season of our national and international history.

In this book, Joseph Mattera gives every Christian a practical theology of the Kingdom. From Chapter 1 through Chapter 10, he builds a compelling argument for why the culture needs us, how our Christianity impels us to act, and the framework for Christian engagement in our culture. More specifically, Dr. Mattera asks important questions of the reader. How are you bearing the image of God within the sphere of influence He has given to you? Is your dream for your life as big as God's dream for you? Or have you short-changed yourself in favor of the comfortable, the familiar, or the safe road?

Once the answers to these questions are revealed, Joseph pushes the button even harder by demonstrating how Christians have abdicated their rightful place in the world's economy, government, business, and society. He convinces us to shake off any lethargy in order to fulfill the covenant God established with Adam to dominate the earth in every possible way. Although the principles of this covenant clash with our culture, Rev. Mattera has created the hope and the possibility that we can fulfill God's purposes...one Christian at a time.

The fundamental power source needed to accomplish our purpose comes from the King of kings. As we relinquish our western mindset and trust in God's sovereignty, we will not only bring the Kingdom to bear throughout the world, but will convince others that the God we worship should be their God as well.

Throughout our journey into our new realm of influence, we must stand on the truth that makes the sharp differentiation between light and darkness, good and evil. As our society has turned our heads toward humanism, we must reprogram ourselves with Kingdom truth.

The Kingdom will influence every aspect of life as we engage in finance, business, and government. Through the prayer of faith and following scriptural principles, we will see an advancement of the Kingdom that makes Islam, Hinduism, cults, and Buddhism look like impotent shadows of the True Faith. As non-violent, spiritual warriors, we must endure the clash of our biblical worldview with the philosophical assumptions and belief systems of our contemporary culture.

Although the battle for the minds of this generation seems hopeless to some, we can win this war by following the prescriptions Joseph Mattera gives us in this book. We are not outmanned, outgunned, outmaneuvered, or out-resourced. We can influence the entire world in a relatively short period of time—if we go with the truths laid out in this book.

Pay close attention to both the content and the pacing of this work. It is not a novel simply to be enjoyed. Additionally, it is not a research book that we should refer to in moments of crisis. It is a game plan that gives specific steps of action. At the end of each chapter, thought-provoking questions are provided for meditation and discussion. Don't just read this book...act on it!

Much has been said about the need for change in politics and cultural discourse today. I am convinced that the cry for change has originated in God's heart. At the same time, I find that the methods and priorities of change being championed by most of our mainline political figures fall short of God's goals as outlined in His Word.

Let's take up the challenge to lead this generation into God's perfect will. God is calling you, the generation needs you, the Word of God is directing you, and now Joseph Mattera is exhorting you to find your voice.

Bishop Harry R. Jackson, Jr.
Senior Pastor, Hope Christian Church
Washington, D.C.
Founder and President, High Impact Leadership Coalition

INTRODUCTION

Be *in* the World, Not *of* the World
It is not enough to focus exclusively on the spiritual, on Bible studies and evangelistic campaigns, while turning a blind eye to the distinctive tensions of contemporary life. We must show the world that Christianity is more than private belief and more than personal salvation. We must show that it is a comprehensive life system that answers all of humanity's age-old questions: Where did I come from? Why am I here? Where am I going? Does life have any meaning or purpose?
—Charles Colson[1]

The persistent lie within our current Church culture says that if we are not working within traditional Church ministry, we are not doing the work of God. How foolish this seems when we look at it from a practical point of view. Not all Christians can be ministers in the Church. Even if we could and did, we would not be following Jesus' life example since He spent most of His ministry time with tax collectors, sinners, and those whom most "orthodox" Jews disdained. Those sinners' lives would not have been transformed if Jesus had only stayed within the walls of the synagogues.

Just like in biblical times, many in our postmodern civilization are not drawn to the Church when they face trouble. The poor and the hurting on the streets aren't attracted to "fire and brimstone" preachers and have tired of the negative connotations that come to mind with the word *Christian*. To those trapped in destructive lifestyles, Christians seem to condemn with their words yet fail to exemplify Kingdom principles with their lives.

It is true that the Bible says we are called to be *in* the world though not *of* the world, but we are also commissioned to *go into all* the world and preach the good news *of God's Kingdom* to *all* creation (see John 17:15-18; Mark 16:15). When Jesus prayed for His disciples and for all of us who would follow, He did not ask the Father to take us out of this world but, rather, to protect us from the evil one through the truth of the Word (see John 17:14-18). What better place to be cultural influencers than in the secular world itself as doctors, lawyers, leaders in public policy, teachers in our public school system, and small group leaders in our places of business.

We must move out of our "church-only" mentality and realize that ministry encompasses all walks of life. Without Christians influencing the world's mind-molding spheres of influence, we will fall short of Christ's Great Commission (see Mark 16:15-20). The earth belongs to the Lord, everything in it and all who live on it (see Ps. 24:1-6). When we choose to separate sacred and secular, stating that our Christianity is only a private religious system rather than a worldview, we miss out on the blessings that God has in store for us.

I believe that any honest reader will ultimately come to understand how the work of the cross of Christ has vast cultural implications. My hope and prayer is that Christians will find the motivation to begin to connect their faith with their calling and fulfill that calling in the marketplace.

Let us journey together through each chapter and learn how to effectively advance the Kingdom of God.

Endnote
1. Charles Colson and Nancy Pearcey, *How Now Shall We Live?* (Carol Stream, IL: Tyndale House, 2004), xi.

CHAPTER 1

IMAGE-BEARERS OF GOD

In order to give credence to the principles presented within this book, I need to start off by sharing some significant occurrences in my life. These particular incidents led me to diligently research the Bible and uncover what has become the foundation for my life, the basis for my teachings, and the focus of my worldview. As I strove to truly understand Scripture and desired to see His will done on earth as it is in Heaven, I began to learn the importance of becoming an image-bearer of God.

At the age of 19, only a few months after my conversion, I began regularly preaching to thousands of riders on the New York City subway trains and the Staten Island Ferry. My desire was to live my life totally for my Lord and Savior and to tell everyone I met what His love had done for me. Within one year, I was part of a mission trip to Turkey, going door-to-door trying to give away Turkish language Bibles and Christian literature to the Muslim populace.

During this time in Turkey, the Iranian revolution led by Ayatollah Khomeini had caused such unrest in that nation that martial law was declared and police with drawn machine guns were stationed at almost every street corner. Because of this unrest, my parents had to sign a release form with the missionary agency acknowledging that they knew that there was an 85 percent chance I would land in a Turkish jail for preaching the Gospel. Not only was I not arrested, but God used our group to reach many Muslims in spite of the impact of martial law on their country.

Off to the Soviet Union

With that experience under my belt, a year later my new bride Joyce and I used our wedding money to finance a six-week ministry trip to the Soviet Union. We arrived right after the Moscow Olympics. As we were praying over the map of the cities we were traveling to, the Lord clearly spoke to us that we were going to experience the most persecution in the city of Kiev because it was where we were going to experience the most fruit.

The trip started off with a bang when my new wife forgot that she had Gospel tracts in her jacket. This led to her being strip-searched when we arrived in Moscow. Russian security then found the 70 Russian Bibles that were stashed in a secret compartment sewn into her dress. They separated us and interrogated us for three hours because we refused to sign a paper written in Russian that neither of us understood.

Finally I barged into the room where they were holding Joyce, fully expecting to find my bride scared and frazzled because she was surrounded by intimidating Russian agents. However, the police were actually relieved that I came in the room and were hoping that I would be able to convince my wife to stop stubbornly refusing to obey them. They left us alone briefly, so we held hands and prayed, and within five minutes we were released and free to rejoin our tour group.

From that point on we went all over Moscow, Leningrad (now "Saint Petersburg"), and Kiev, preaching the Gospel to hundreds of English-speaking university students. Some even helped interpret for us as we preached to the crowds who were curious about life in the West. At that time the Russian officials were attempting to stop all contact between their people and western media sources, not even allowing us to bring in a western newspaper or magazine.

Therefore most of what the Russian people learned about the West was through personal contact with tourists or by listening to the radio show, "The Voice of America."

Along with those hungry for information about the western world, students who were spies for the KGB constantly followed us. We needed a word from the Lord every day to know who we could trust to interpret and help us share the Gospel. We did not work with the underground Church because our goal was to preach the Gospel in the main city centers to non-Christian university students.

In Leningrad my wife began to experience severe abdominal pain and was admitted to a dingy hospital where they wanted to perform surgery on her to remove her appendix. We knew in our hearts that this was a misdiagnosis, so after three days of trying to convince them to release her, I went into the hospital in the middle of the night to sneak her out. In spite of all these trials, many people in the streets and universities heard the Gospel for the first time as God continually guided our steps.

When we arrived in Kiev, the Lord supernaturally connected us with other American pastors who furnished us with Russian Bibles to give to a number of students as we led them to the Lord. One day, after noticing that those we had been ministering to stopped showing up for their discipleship appointments, we realized we were being followed by the KGB. This frustrated us because we couldn't preach the Gospel while these three men in black suits tailed us. I told my wife that we would not leave the hotel room again until the Lord told us it was the right time.

So we prayed in our hotel room for hours until the Lord said, "Go." We went downstairs as the maid on our hotel floor called down to the front desk to alert the KGB waiting out front of the hotel. But this time, as soon as we walked into the lobby, a huge truckload of hundreds of bags of luggage pulled up in front of the hotel, momentarily blocking the view of the KGB officers waiting out front.

This gave us a few seconds to jump on a public bus that just happened to be passing by at that moment. That day we were able to preach to multitudes of people before the KGB showed up in the public square looking for us. But even as they began to search the crowd for us, God blinded them and they didn't recognize us even though I was clearly preaching the Gospel message. We were able to continue preaching all day and into the night to hungry students and passersby as God supernaturally intervened on our behalf.

When this successful trip was over and we were ready to fly out of Kiev to Moscow en route to New York City, the flight attendant attempted to stop us from getting on the plane. After receiving a word of wisdom from the Lord, I took Joyce's hand and boldly walked up to the flight attendant at the top of the portable stairs leading to the entrance of the plane, pretending I had to ask her a question. Instead of stopping to speak to her, we pushed her out of the way and walked right onto the plane.

We took our seats and looked out the window to see the plane surrounded by black limousines and men in black suits speaking on walkie-talkies. We prayed, and the Lord gave us the Scripture in Matthew 10:28, *"Do not fear those who kill the body but are unable to kill the soul..."* (NASB). We had peace about the situation, and within minutes the authorities decided not to make a scene in front of all the other American tourists. Our plane took off for Moscow as scheduled.

Sacred Versus Secular

When we got back to New York City in September of 1980, the Lord impressed upon my heart that I was to evangelize full-time and that He would supply all of our financial needs. For the next three years, all I did was wander the streets, personally and publicly ministering to others. We even closed down a number of blocks in our community to show Christian films that resulted in hundreds of people making a decision to follow Christ. In 1984, our pastor sent us out to plant a church to more effectively evangelize and minister to our community.

Unfortunately, during this time, my perspective regarding God's Kingdom was very narrow. I thought that His Kingdom was primarily relegated to the spiritual realm with occasional manifestations of the miraculous, like answering prayer or healing the sick.

Without knowing it, I had fallen into a belief system that asserts that the material world is evil and that the highest good can only be fulfilled through spiritual things. I was also constantly looking to the future, expecting the Rapture and the imminent return of our Lord rather than focusing on how I could be a practical minister of Christ to those around me in my everyday life.

Consequently, up until 1995, I had to fight my guilt-ridden conscience when I read the newspaper, studied current events, or delved deeply into editorials and political commentaries. I felt uneasy if I read anything other than the Bible, Church history, or overtly Christian writings like apologetics. In reflection, I realize that I was interested in politics and public policy because, as a leader, I innately understood that these arenas of life were vitally important for all people, irrespective of whether or not they were Christians.

I had this innate desire to understand economics, political science, and great literature, and to admire art and music. But I did not have a belief system that could sustain or justify these desires since they were supposedly secular and not sacred. I had been taught that earthly interests were a waste of time because the antichrist would be coming soon to take over the world and the Rapture was about to happen. Therefore, the only thing that really mattered was winning souls for Christ.

Even though I was very narrow-minded, a noteworthy result stemmed from those years in my life: I became thoroughly familiar with the Scriptures, Church history, and apologetics. The problem was that I wasn't able to apply all of that knowledge in any manner that would positively influence those outside of the Christian world. This left me feeling like there had to be more to life as a Christian than hoarding this knowledge behind church doors.

The Real Kingdom

In 1995 and 1996, a few things converged together, totally changing my perspective on what it meant to live in and for the Kingdom of God. In the spring of 1995, I sat under a historian named Dr. Raymond Bakke, who had come to speak at a one-day event for Christian leaders in New York City. For the first time in my life, I heard a person eloquently teach with passion and authority about effective urban ministry. He challenged us to have a theology as big as our city. He spoke about taking the whole Gospel to the whole person and explained the need to not only exegete the Scriptures, but also exegete our communities.

Exegesis of Scripture has to do with drawing out the intended meaning from the original languages as well as from the historical and cultural context of the passage. Hence, to exegete a community means to draw on all available sources for relevant information so as to minister to others in a way that they can understand and from which they can benefit the most.

Dr. Bakke also told us that pastors are called to not only shepherd their local congregation, but to also shepherd their community. He quoted one author after another in the areas of sociology, economics, and history, without overtly quoting from or waving his Bible. I was totally flabbergasted.

Never in my life had I heard a Christian minister teach with so much practical and intellectual authority. A chord that had been dormant in my heart for 18 years finally resonated within me. For the first time in my life, I felt like I had permission from God to combine my biblical knowledge with an intellectual pursuit of knowledge that would have practical application to earth's current reality.

I began to realize that the Bible held the key to unlocking all truth, not just religious truth. Instantaneously both my theological lens and my understanding of responsibility regarding Christian stewardship expanded. I no longer had a Gospel that was limited to saving individual souls from hell; rather, it also included a mandate to steward the earth as salt and light. I began to see that the Kingdom of God involved His whole created order, not just the spiritual realm.

After Dr. Bakke finished speaking, I approached him like a man dying of thirst in the desert, practically begging him for more resources and information so I could get started on this new journey with God. The result of this meeting was nothing short of a paradigm transformation! I started devouring every book about urban ministry, community development, social reform, economics, and world history that I could get my hands on.

It was such an obsession that one national leader I knew told me I needed to take a leave of absence as pastor of my local church so that I could attend seminary and get this all out of my system. He told me that it was just new revelation and that it would eventually wear off. But more than a decade later, my obsession has only increased, although it is more focused now as I work toward my second doctorate degree.

Soon after this event, I was invited to a week-long theological and historical discussion with reformed theologians and academicians. During this experience, these scholars recommended books and introduced concepts that further enhanced my theological journey regarding the relevance of the Gospel for both redemption and our stewardship of creation.

Moral Decline in America

I was also continuing my study of Church history and began to notice that, prior to the Civil War, most of the American Church was influenced by Puritan Reformed theology. They preached that the Kingdom of God was to be manifested on the earth by applying the Bible to law, civil government, education, and public policy in general. This, among other things, produced the founding documents of our nation: the Declaration of Independence and the Constitution.

Nine of the 13 Ivy League schools, including Harvard, Yale, King's College (now Columbia University), and Princeton, were intricately involved in the development of the social and political fabric of our nation. Their leaders taught and applied the Bible to every aspect of their lives on earth, not just to the spiritual world to come.

However, after the Civil War, people lost hope in God and in our Christian society. Perhaps it was the horror of seeing more than 600,000 people die. Perhaps it was the fact that some of our nation's early Christian leaders had embraced slavery. Whatever the reason, the Church lost her passion to establish the Kingdom of God in America.

This opened the door to an escapist theology in which people lived for the future rather than for the present. The present seemed too difficult for them so they focused forward, watching for the coming of the antichrist, eagerly anticipating Christ's return, and longing for the Rapture and the day they would leave this earth and enter Heaven.

I realized that often our theology and eschatology (beliefs about the end of the world) are more influenced by our circumstances and sociopolitical environment than by the Bible. Consequently, we can look back and see that Christianity began losing its foothold in our culture from the 1880s to the 1980s.

This awareness pushed me over the edge. My reasoning has always been that every teaching that is blessed by God bears good fruit. The new theological emphasis that had emerged after the Civil War resulted in churches abandoning the secular culture. This abandonment coincided with the moral decline of America. Because this was the fruit I had witnessed, I felt that the escapist theology could not be biblically sound.

Since these events of 1995, the Gospel has made so much more sense to me. I have come to realize that Scripture never divides sacred from secular. The Bible is a practical book that primarily emphasizes a believer's responsibility to be a steward of the earth.

This gives even more relevance to the cross, the nature and mission of the Church, and the role of Jesus the Anointed One as King of kings and Lord of lords over His Kingdom. Jesus' title, "King of kings," implies that He is the President over all presidents, the Prime Minister over all prime ministers, and the Prince over all princes. Hence, the present-day ministry of Christ and of His followers should include politics and public policy.

Scripture brilliantly combines things in Heaven with things on the earth (see Eph. 1:10) and encourages all believers, whether they function in full-time ministry or not, to be released as practical ministers of the Kingdom of God on the earth. I finally came to realize that *"the earth is the Lord's..."* (Ps. 24:1) and that it doesn't belong to the devil.

Therefore, my call as a believer is to extend His Kingdom influence into every realm of society. A powerful sense of purpose began to permeate every area of my life as I realized the depth and reality of the Great Commission that Jesus has given to each and every Christian.

I also began to understand just how vitally important it is for us to learn how to truly reflect His image no matter where we are or what we are doing.

Reflecting His Image

At the writing of this book, I have been married 28 years and am the father of five children. I have always made spending time with my children a high priority and have given precedence to biblical teaching. As they've gotten older, I've not only taught my children typical Bible stories, but have also discussed with them how to apply the principles found within these stories to every area of life so they will see their lives through biblical lenses. One of the most important guidelines I've given to them is to "think biblically, but speak secularly."

Because of my perspective on the Kingdom of God, I have never pushed any of my five children to serve in full-time, church-related ministry. I kept their unique identities in mind as I trained them biblically, knowing that each of them is called to reflect God's image in their own particular way.

Although my oldest son Jason preaches in various Christian conferences, he is not primarily called to the church realm, but to the marketplace, specifically to the media. I expect him to continue to have quite an impact on secular culture even though I, his father, am primarily called to the church.

Out of my five biological children, quite possibly only two are called to full-time ecclesial ministry. The others are called to the arts, business, and other fields. I do hope, however, that each of them will receive a theological education along with their business education because of its practical application to all other realms of their lives.

Having a desire to serve God and reflect His image is as innate in us as breathing air. When the Kingdom of God is proclaimed through humanity, it is powerful because it evokes what already metaphysically exists in the hearts of all people: our purpose and destiny. When the Body of Christ finally grasps this, local congregations will begin to nurture the best and the brightest of the top mind-molders of society.

I can see a day in the future when the world will be coming to the Church for ideas on caring for creation and environmental issues. Politicians will seek advice on public policy regarding the formulation of curriculum for and administration of urban educational systems and on how to redevelop communities that have been left for dead.

I envision a day when Christians will write and produce the most compelling theatrical productions and the greatest novels and movies that explore and understand humanity better than anything Hollywood has ever produced. The future Church will once again penetrate culture by producing the world's greatest artists, musicians, composers, architects, political leaders, entrepreneurs, venture capitalists, and even lending institutions.

Presently we see a taste of this as many Christian authors have made inroads with secular book publishing companies and marketing. For example, I regularly see books by John Maxwell and T.D. Jakes in airport bookstores across the nation. Also of note are the inroads that contemporary Christian music has made into the mainstream music and media industry. This past year I even saw two *American Idol* shows that featured inspirational Christian music that mirrored a Sunday worship service.

In addition to this, the past few decades have seen a resurgence of evangelicals involved in the political, sociology, and philosophy spheres. If more pulpits enunciated the Kingdom message, we would see our churches teeming with the best and brightest emergent leaders that the world has ever seen.

I believe the days of the evangelical, fundamentalist approach that includes a pharisaical separation from the world is coming to an end in this needy 21st century. Congregations built only on preaching and choirs will soon become the new dinosaurs. Only Christians who understand that there is no distinction between secular and sacred will truly impact our world for His Kingdom.

God First

You may have heard the advice given to Christians that they are to make God first, ministry second, family third, and work or vocation last when prioritizing their lives. I believe instead that Christians are to embrace the idea of God being involved in every aspect of human life. When God is first in our ministry, first in our family, and first in our vocation, we don't have to wonder if we are giving God enough focus in our lives.

Jesus said to seek first the Kingdom of God and His way of doing things, and when we do that, everything else that we need will automatically fall into place (see Matt. 6:33). The apostle Peter said that God's divine power has given us everything we need for a life of godliness through His very great and precious promises (see 2 Pet. 1:3-4).

Many evangelicals believe that the first move of the Holy Spirit on the earth was on the Day of Pentecost, but even a cursory reading of the Book of Genesis illustrates that the Holy Spirit was moving upon the face of the earth immediately after Creation (see Gen. 1:1-3). He has been the epitome of creativity since the very beginning; thus the Holy Spirit is attracted to the divine creativity in man.

If you are called by God to be an artist, then you should expect the Holy Spirit to smile and move upon you while you are painting a canvas, not just when you are praying or worshipping in church. You should feel free to fully be yourself, embracing the way God made you and flowing with the prompting of the Holy Spirit to impact your area of influence.

Furthermore, the first instance of the gifts of the Holy Spirit empowering a person in the Bible is not in the New Testament. It is when the Spirit of God came upon Bezalel to grant him skill, ability, and knowledge of all kinds of crafts. The Spirit empowered him to make artistic designs in gold, silver, and bronze; to cut and set stones; to work in wood; and to engage in all kinds of craftsmanship for the building of the tabernacle of Moses (see Exod. 31:1-5). God has placed talents and abilities in each of us so that we can help build and expand His Kingdom here on the earth. We certainly won't have need of them in Heaven.

Transforming Culture

When our Christian worldview is big enough to include God in everything we do, even the darkest places in our world will be transformed by His truth. If we do not realize what the Great Commission is really calling us to accomplish with our lives, many emerging leaders will either fall short of their cultural calling or attempt to express their gifts only within the safe walls of the Christian community.

Jesus commissioned us to go into *all* the world and transform it through preaching the good news to *all* creation. He promised that if we would go forth as His image-bearers, then signs and wonders would accompany us and confirm His Word spoken through us (see Mark 16:15-20).

THINK ON THIS

How is the message of the Kingdom of God resonating in your mind and heart as you read these pages?

How are you planning to obey the Christian calling to transform culture as an image-bearer of God?

To aid in this process, ask yourself the following questions and journal your thoughts. Then ask God what He thinks about the answers you've given. You can trust Him to guide and lead you to the freedom you need to accomplish all that He has for you, whether it is inside or outside the Church.

Do you have recurring dreams of doing something great in this world but have pushed them aside because they didn't fit within the confines of your local church?

Do you have certain desires regarding art, music composition, dance, theater, writing, etc., that you have pushed down inside of you because those gifts are not being celebrated in your local congregation?

Do you feel called to be a Christian leader, yet you don't feel a passion to be in full-time church ministry?

As you go through the chapters of this book, God may expand on the things you have written in your journal. Keep it handy and add to it as you progress through each phase of this material. By the time you finish this book, you should have some clear direction on what God would have you do to become an effective image-bearer in the Kingdom of God on the earth.

CHAPTER 2
CHRISTIANITY AND CULTURE

Society, like the church, is an organism, not just an aggregate of individuals; no person exists as an isolated individual. Man, as the divine image-bearer, must respect the spheres of authority God has ordained, and the state must assure the just operation of those spheres. —Abraham Kuyper[1]

In this chapter I will give an overview of some of the salient issues regarding the Church's relationship to culture and the spheres of authority mentioned in the quote above. We will grapple with the proper roles of the Church, civic government, the cultural commission, and the various jurisdictions of society. I will expound on the fact that Christians need to have a biblical worldview in order to fulfill their leadership function in society.

By studying history and tracking cultural changes and the influence of Christianity on various types of sociological structures, we can gain valuable insight on what has or has not been effective in the past. We can discover what God's people need to do to bring about a balance of power between the two major influences in today's world events.

Imbalance

Human history gives us many examples of abuse of power by an individual, a religious institution, or a centrally controlled state government. Even 20th-century history is replete with tyrannical political leaders such as Hitler of Germany, Pol Pot of Cambodia, Idi Amin of Uganda, Mao Zedong of China, and Joseph Stalin of Russia. To a lesser degree, some would even include recent Russian president Vladimir Putin in this infamous list.

These unscrupulous leaders concentrated power under their rule in such a way that they were able to take the lives of millions of innocent people whom they perceived as a threat to their rule or societal philosophy.

The communist revolutions under Lenin of the Soviet Union and Zedong of China were attempts to overthrow every ideological system that appeared as a threat to their absolute control of their respective geographic areas. Consequently, during those reigns of power, church buildings and Bibles were destroyed, pastors were imprisoned or martyred, and children became wards of the state.

We have also seen examples of religious tyranny as we study Church history. The infamous Spanish Inquisition of the Roman Catholic Church several hundred years ago resulted in the deaths of thousands of people who didn't conform doctrinally to official Roman Catholic teachings. The Salem witch trials of the 17th century saw numerous people burned to death by the New England Puritans.

Most recently we see an Islamic fundamentalist rule in nations like Saudi Arabia and Iran in which Sharia law, based on an interpretation of Quranic law, is integrated with the national, political, and economic systems. These government-enforced religious laws allow husbands to have multiple wives and concubines, condone physical abuse of the women in these "harems," and require all women to cover virtually every part of their body.

These are only a few examples of the unfortunate consequences that cultures experience when either the state government or a particular religious institution or denomination exercises too much power and violates the boundaries of other spheres of society. To effectively prevent such abuse of power, we need to gain an understanding of God's perspective on the role of Christianity in society.

When we examine Scripture, we find that there are five distinct realms of society that God has ordained to reflect His Kingdom jurisdictions on earth. For now let's begin our quest for truth by discovering what God's definition of government really is.

Defining Government

To show how much our culture has changed in its concept of government, we need to read the definition given in Noah Webster's 1828 version of the *American Dictionary of the English Language*. In that book, the first two definitions under the word *government* have to do with people exercising *self-control* over their own tempers and passions and in regard to their overall personal conduct.

If we use today's Internet superhighway to seek a contemporary definition of government, we discover that it is now defined as "the organization that is the governing authority of a political unit, the ruling power in a political society, and the apparatus through which a governing body functions and exercises authority."[2]

Hence, we can see just by its usage in the common vernacular that the realm of self-government has been virtually replaced by the notion that government should be a collection of political leaders who control every aspect of our life and culture.

We have been so brainwashed by the socialistic concept of a big civic government that the vast majority would define *government* as the political organization over their city, state, or country that is supposed to provide protection and ensure that all their needs are met.

I have been in evangelical churches all over this country, and when I ask Christians what they think of when I say the word *government,* inevitably almost 100 percent will mention the name of a political leader. Unfortunately it seems the Church has been just as influenced by this false definition of government as the secular world.

The first question we must ask ourselves is: What is God's definition of government? God's original design revealed in Scripture clearly shows five macro jurisdictions (or governments) of society:

1. **Personal Jurisdiction:** Individuals are responsible to govern their own lives in accordance with the laws of sowing and reaping (see Gal. 6:7-10).

2. **Family Jurisdiction:** Parents are primarily responsible to raise and educate their children (see Deut. 6:7; Prov. 4:1; Eph. 5:1-6:4).

3. **Business Jurisdiction (or voluntary associations):** People are allowed to be involved in business and to own private property (see Exod. 20:17; Isa. 65:21-22).

4. **Ecclesial Jurisdiction (or religious):** Churches should be free to preach the Gospel (see Matt. 28:18-20; Acts 4:18-20).

5. **Civic or Political Jurisdiction:** The people and/or groups in this jurisdiction should provide order and safety so the other four jurisdictions of society can function in peace and safety (see Rom. 13:1-7; 1 Tim. 2:1-4).

Each of these five jurisdictions were created by God to supplement—not supplant—each other. The church is called to train and release servant leaders who will influence every one of these realms as Salt and Light (see Eph. 4:10; Matt. 5:13-16).

In cases where one of these jurisdictions acts irresponsibly or immorally, the others may have the right to step in and take away its freedom. For example, if parents don't care for their children, the state has the right to take away their children. If an individual commits a crime, the state has the right to put that person in jail. In history we have also seen examples where one of these jurisdictions unbiblically supplant one or more of the other jurisdictions—as when the church violated individual freedom when they persecuted and even killed non-believers (during the Inquisition).

The Cultural Commission

The order of balance that society should have between sacred and secular is one of ongoing debate. Obviously the Bible is very clear on certain aspects of responsibility, such as helping the poor and providing for widows. But the question remains as to how the Kingdom of Heaven should be manifested in the earth's government while fulfilling these and other mandates spelled out in Scripture.

Those favoring the Christian socialist side believe that the state and federal government should be large, regulate all societal activity, and leverage taxes to help the poor. Those who are more conservative believe in a small local state and federal government whose primary role is to keep order in society, leaving the responsibility of aiding the poor primarily to their biological families and local religious institutions. So which view is correct according to God's instructions to His representatives here on the earth?

When thinking through issues related to the role of Christians in civil government and society, we need to use as our starting point the fact that God gave man a distinct Cultural Commission in Genesis 1:28 (NIV):

> *God blessed them and said to them, "Be fruitful and increase in number; fill the earth and subdue it. Rule over the fish of the sea and the birds of the air and over every living creature that moves on the ground."*

This mandate shows that God called those in covenant with Him to be involved in the stewardship of the whole earth. God did not, however, make a so-called "sacred and secular" divide, but instructed His covenant people to subdue and have dominion over *all* of the created order on the earth. That is to say, we are called by God to establish and frame *all* of the different aspects of civilization. (True biblical dominion comes by servant leadership—not by forcing people to obey Old Testament civil laws and enacting Old Testament punishment for breaking said laws.)

A point of clarification here: *when God says **all**, He means **all**.* According to this initial Cultural Commission, God's *all* not only includes religion, but also civil law and *all* of its processes as well. This means that as Christians our realm of responsibility encompasses education, health care, economics, business, art, anthropology, zoology, botany, nutrition, and *all* other aspects of creation care, including protecting the environment. Those who recognize themselves as image-bearers of God should mimic His creativity and become the leading thinkers and practitioners in *all* of these various areas of concern. To be "heavenly minded" should always translate to becoming "earthly good."

Jesus gave us the New Testament equivalent of the Cultural Commission in Matthew 28:19-20 (NIV):

*Therefore go and make disciples of **all** nations, baptizing them in the name of the Father and of the Son and of the Holy Spirit, and teaching them to obey **everything** I have commanded you....*

Jesus instructs us to apply God's spiritual and social Kingdom principles to *every* realm of our present world system as we follow His directive to disciple *"all* nations." Thus Scripture teaches that God's ultimate goal for nations is for Christians to operate in high levels of influence in culture for the glory of Christ, which would militate against the belief in a large, central political government that penetrates and regulates all of life by assuming a god-like place by attempting to provide for the needs of all its citizens.

For the past 100 years, most of the evangelical community have misinterpreted the phrase *"disciple all nations."* They mistakenly deem it to mean that individual ethnicities and groups of people should be discipled within each nation.

But those who grasp this commission's true meaning realize that this verse is referring to the Church continually being involved in the cultural transformation of *all* aspects of the culture in *all* nations. Therefore, the Church is called to disciple *whole* people groups or nations, utilizing the *entire* Bible as a blueprint for framing the created order.

This commission also includes the responsibility of directly influencing the civil governments of each of these nations with His Kingdom principles. (Even in a pluralistic society, Christians should be able to present significant ideas that enhance the quality of life for all.)

In our discussion concerning Christianity's involvement in these various influential aspects of society and culture, it is important not to disregard Old Testament teachings. Matthew 5:17-19 teaches that Jesus didn't come to abolish the law, but to fulfill it. In Matthew 28:19, He commissioned us to disciple the nations by teaching them *everything* He had commanded.

Many theologians believe that Old Testament law is divided into three components: ceremonial law, moral law, and civic law. In order to fully understand God's plan, we must know how the components of Old Testament law are applicable today, especially in the realms of moral and civil law. (This will be more fully developed in my next book.)

The Old Testament in fact exemplifies the necessary blueprint for discipling nations and manifesting Kingdom influence on modern society. We need to develop a biblical worldview, implementing truths from the whole Bible, in order to fulfill this Great Commission as it is given to us through both Old and New Testament principles.

Developing a Biblical Worldview

If the Bible was meant merely for the individual's salvation and spiritual formation, then the Old Testament teachings regarding economics and civil law were only relevant to the Jewish people before Christ. But if Matthew 28:19-20 refers to the Church being called to use the Scriptures to teach nations to obey everything He commanded, then the Old Testament economic and civic principles should be used as a blueprint for developing and advancing the culture of people groups and their societies today as well.

The role of the Church then is to train and equip believers to take leadership roles in every facet of society by giving them a biblical worldview in whatever discipline or vocation to which they are called. This was the primary reason why Christians established Ivy League schools such as Harvard, Yale, King's College, Princeton, and Dartmouth.

However, encouraging Christians to participate as leaders in the various aspects of our culture is much different than saying that one particular church or denomination should be the ruling political entity of that society. Although the Church is called to disciple the nations, the ecclesial or church realm should not try to force all the other realms to be under its immediate jurisdiction.

We are called instead to go and make disciples of all the members of the society or culture we are living, working, and playing in. To influence modern society, it is imperative that we, as Christians and disciples of Christ, understand the philosophies of the culture we are called to disciple in His name.

Postmodernism

One of the most prevalent and challenging philosophies the church has to grapple with is postmodernism because it is so diametrically opposed to absolutes, and thus opposed to the biblical worldview.

If we are going to be effective in regards to discipling our particular sphere of influence, it is imperative for us to understand how postmodernism is affecting the Church and every aspect of the global world around us. The most direct effect of postmodernism on society today is that truth is being challenged at nearly every level.

Christians need to be taught and then stand by God's truth in order to impact our world and carry out the Cultural Commission to create a culture reflective of God's Kingdom.

Some Christian practitioners and scholars argue against the effectiveness of trying to present a biblical view of life because of the influence of this postmodern mindset on our society. Those adhering to this postmodern belief system feel that there is no absolute truth. Instead, truth is relative to what they believe or feel at any given moment and is totally dependent on their particular set of circumstances. This has resulted in a society that says, "If it feels good, do it" and believes that nothing is sin if the individual feels it is right based on his or her circumstances.

Rather than retreating from the challenges of presenting a cohesive biblical view of the world as reflected by the Kingdom of God, Christians should be trained to effectively illustrate how a postmodern approach to life is impossible. Denying absolutes means that one must also deny the law of noncontradiction. According to Aristotle, the law of noncontradiction is the principle that "opposite assertions cannot be true at the same time." For example, a mathematical equation like 2+2 can never equal 4 *and* 5 at the same time, no matter what the surrounding circumstances might be.

Another effective way to approach people with this mindset is to point out that a true adherent of this postmodern mindset should be willing to be slapped in the face or robbed without objecting or saying that it is wrong if the perpetrator argues that his actions were a good thing or made him feel good.

Solid examples such as these clearly demonstrate that there are indeed absolute laws, and they show that the postmodernist is actually having to consistently borrow from a morally absolute worldview in order to function normally in modern society. Their use of mathematical formulations and concepts of good and evil are in fact an oxymoron in light of their attempts to deny the existence of absolute concepts.

Learning how to biblically and intellectually counter the principles that have created a postmodern mindset allows us to more effectively infiltrate and bring about change in this misguided cultural structure.

In researching this subject, I found that Douglas Groothuis explains some of the reasons for the rise of postmodernism in his book *Truth Decay*. Understanding what caused the gravitation to this mindset in the first place will help us more effectively counteract it as we begin to present God's truth to those imbedded in this misinformed "modern" culture.

1. The social situation of people in a cosmopolitan, media-saturated environment makes a unified worldview untenable; the tie between information and human purpose has been severed. Information appears indiscriminately, directed at no one in particular, in enormous volume and at high speeds, and disconnected from theory, meaning, or purpose.

2. The diversity of religious and philosophical perspectives available to people today makes the notion of one absolutely true religion or philosophy unacceptable.

3. Cosmopolitan and pluralistic environments do not allow for a fixed sense of personal identity or one best way of life.[3]

If we are going to be effective in regards to discipling *all* nations and influencing *all* cultures, it is imperative for us to understand how postmodernism as well as other cultural mindsets are affecting the Church and the global world culture.

I will deal more with such individual mindsets in Chapter 10, "The Clash of Worldviews." But for now, embrace the truth that God has called us to be His ambassadors, His personal representatives in every facet of daily life (see 2 Cor. 5:16-20).

As His image-bearers, we are to directly influence our portion of the earth and aspire to not only repeat the prayer that Jesus taught us in Luke 11:2-3, but to actively work to see it fulfilled through each of our lives. As you speak the words of this prayer out loud, listen to what you are really saying and begin to truly mean what you say. *"Our Father in heaven, hallowed be Your name, **Your kingdom come. Your will be done on earth as it is in heaven"*** (Luke 11:2 NKJV).

Think Biblically, but Speak Secularly

When my oldest son Jason attended a secular college, he took my teaching seriously. Within three months he became the leader of the college's rather dormant Republican Club, subsequently influencing about 30 students to join. He began his own school newspaper and had his own weekly radio show that went out to the whole state of Rhode Island every Saturday for three hours.

Then he used the political club to train student activists, used the newspaper to print articles that countered the far-left liberal propaganda imbuing the school, and used the radio show to debate so-called experts about current events and salient ideological issues.

Jason eventually gained stewardship over the student finances as a member of the Student Senate and used his influence to bring in high-level conservative speakers who attracted large crowds and stirred up the cultural waters of this college campus. His impact on the school was so vast that a number of far-left liberal professors actually asked the president of the school to graduate my son one year early so as to eliminate his powerful influence.

When he did graduate, he was offered a job as the Public Relations Director of a large conservative organization. Since the age of 21, he has regularly been on national television discussing such culturally relevant topics as foreign policy, the economy, presidential elections, and other important policy items.

It all comes back to the strategy I taught and exemplified for him as he was growing up. A Christian can positively influence society for the Kingdom of God by "thinking biblically, but speaking secularly."

THINK ON THIS

As we conclude this chapter on Christianity and its relationship to culture, take a moment to reflect on the principles I have presented: imbalances in power between different institutions like the church and state, the concept of government, the five macro jurisdictions of the Kingdom, the role of the Church in culture, and the need for Christians to have a biblical worldview.

Ask yourself the following questions and journal your thoughts.

Were any of the principles new to your way of thinking?

If so, which ones and how are they different?

What was your definition of "government" before you read this chapter?

What is your perspective on government now?

What are the five macro jurisdictions of a society?

What is the role of the church in these jurisdictions?

How are these principles going to affect the way you fulfill the Great Commission?

Endnotes

1. James Edward McGoldrick, *God's Renaissance Man: Abraham Kuyper* (Darlington, England: Evangelical Press, 2000), 80.

2. *Wikipedia*, s.v. "government," http://en.wikipedia.org/wiki/Government#cite_note-0 (accessed March 26, 2009).

3. Douglas Groothuis, *Truth Decay: Defending Christianity Against the Challenges of Postmodernism* (Downers Grove, IL: InterVarsity Press, 2000), 26-30.

CHAPTER 3
THE COVENANTS OF THE KINGDOM

*Then God said, "Let us make man in Our image, in Our like-
ness, and let them rule over the fish of the sea and the birds of
the air, over the livestock, over all the earth, and over all the
creatures that move along the ground." So God created man in
His own image, in the image of God He created him; male and
female He created them.* **God blessed them and said to them,
"Be fruitful and increase in number; fill the earth and
subdue it. Rule over the fish of the sea and the birds of
the air and over every living creature that moves on the
ground"** *(Genesis 1:26-28 NIV).*

Genesis 1:28 is the cornerstone and starting point in which
we find our calling as God's people. This Cultural Commission is strewn throughout every covenant and dispensation from Genesis to Revelation, connecting the Old and New
Testaments. We cannot comprehend the purpose of the cross and
the mission of Christ if we do not understand the connection between Genesis 1:28 and the instructions of Jesus in Matthew
28:18-20:

*Then Jesus came to them and said, "All authority in heaven
and on earth has been given to Me. Therefore go and make*

disciples of all nations, baptizing them in the name of the Father and of the Son and of the Holy Spirit, and teaching them to obey everything I have commanded you. And surely I am with you always, to the very end of the age" (NIV).

The Church is not called to wait until Christ comes back to begin to subdue His enemies under His feet. We are called to be the primary agent through whom He extends His rule over the nations (see Ps. 2:8; 110:1-2).

Thus, the mystery of God presently revealed in the New Testament is that His will is to bring all things together in Christ, both in Heaven and on earth (see Eph. 1:9-11). Unless there is a theological transformation in our understanding of the Cultural Commission, we will never witness societal transformation in our present world.

Through my research and studies, I have come to understand that the Bible is primarily a covenant document or a legal treatise based on God's law. I believe that Scripture cannot be properly understood or interpreted unless the covenantal structure is illuminated to us.

Therefore, I have dedicated this chapter to showing *how* we can restore ourselves and our communities to fully honor the original covenant that God gave to us in Genesis 1:28. Once we do, we can walk in the fullness of God's blessings and reflect His Kingdom on earth as it is in Heaven as we pray Luke 11:2-3 over our spheres of influence.

The Importance of Covenant

Consider the following story about a young woman who came to know God on a personal level after a near-death experience. After surrendering her life to Him, she reflected on the change that was necessary to live righteously and find the peace and happiness she had always desired.

Before the accident, her life had been filled with parties, alcohol, boyfriends, and materialism, but she knew that she could no longer participate in these actions. Therefore she began to eliminate her old behaviors. She even prayed that God would restore her physically—that God would heal her body so that she would have a new hymen, the beautiful symbol of the blood covenant when a man and woman come together in marriage. Then she remained celibate until her marriage seven years later.

On the third night after her wedding, she bled. She did not bleed on the first night, as she would have done had she been a virgin. It was as if God was saying to her that through the Trinity she was reconciled back into a covenant of purity both to God and to her husband. She cried when she realized that God had answered her prayer and that God thought it important enough to restore her hymen so that she and her husband might have a symbol of covenant for their union.[1]

In His grace, God's forgiveness extends into our repentance and our desire to live righteously. As you can already see, the importance of covenant cannot be overstated. God takes covenant seriously.

Nothing to Mess With

In the true story shared above, we witness the magnitude of importance that God gives to covenants, especially covenantal relationships. They are not to be taken lightly, overlooked, or broken. A broken covenant echoes drastic consequences, not only for the covenant-breakers but also for their families and communities even in subsequent generations. An unbroken covenant, however, brings life and prosperity. Deuteronomy 8:18 teaches us that God wants to prosper His people so they can confirm His covenant on the earth.

Before we get into a detailed study of the Scriptures regarding covenant, let's make sure we have a foundational understanding of what covenant means. The word *covenant* in its most basic form simply means "to cut." The phrase "to cut the covenant" signifies two people or entities making an agreement with each other and sealing it with the shedding of blood.

Besides the obvious illustration of covenant between a husband and wife that is mentioned above, covenant has been practiced throughout history by people cutting themselves and mingling their blood, such as when Native Americans became "blood brothers."

During Old Testament times, it was common practice that when a covenant was established, an animal was cut in half and both parties walked between the pieces in the form of a figure eight while reciting the blessings of keeping covenant and the curses or consequences for breaking it.

Because the Bible is primarily a covenantal document, we see an illustration of this custom when God made a covenant with Abraham and his descendants. He ratified it by manifesting as a flaming torch and walking in between the pieces of the animal Abraham had cut in half (see Gen. 15:9-19). God can swear by no one greater than Himself; no one else could guarantee the fulfillment of that redemptive covenant, so He became the sole assurance.[2]

Not only were covenants a normal part of God's interaction with His people, but so were the blessings of obedience and the curses of disobedience. Deuteronomy 29:9 teaches that prosperity comes only by obedience to the covenant. In Deuteronomy 27:12-28, the heads of half of the tribes of Israel stood on Mount Gerizim to pronounce the blessings of obedience to God's commands while the other half stood on Mount Ebal to pronounce the curses for disobedience.

Starting with the Exodus from Egypt, the children of Israel connected to God and kept covenant with Him primarily by obeying the ceremonial and moral laws that had been revealed to Moses. The Ten Commandments are called a covenant in Deuteronomy 4:13. Four of the first five books of the Old Testament are dedicated to explicating the detail and application of the Ten Commandments through civil and ceremonial law. Moses was so identified with this national covenant with God that it was eventually known as "the law of Moses" (Luke 24:44).

Modern-Day Covenants

Covenants are to the Kingdom of God what the United States Constitution is to America. They elucidate every major aspect of the role of the King of the Kingdom, His representatives, and how Kingdom citizens are to live for historical continuity.

A biblical covenant involves transcendence, representation, ethical stipulations, consequences for obedience or disobedience, and generational continuity. Scripture frequently teaches that keeping covenant with God is the key to dominion and the fulfillment of the Cultural Commission in Genesis 1:28 (see also Deut. 28:11; Ps. 78). Consequently, breaking covenant unleashes curses such as sickness, fatigue, and death on the disobedient (see 1 Cor. 11:17-34).

Although outside of Scripture there aren't many modern-day covenants that exactly reflect the biblical pattern, I will give some contemporary examples to better illustrate this concept. I will start with the typical Christian union between a man and a woman in holy matrimony. Traditionally, marriage vows are close to the biblical pattern because they involve making a covenant before God. Through this act, God's transcendence as judge and witness of these vows is displayed. The man and the woman are given an understanding of the conditional blessings of this covenantal agreement. If there is faithfulness in the marriage, they receive the blessings of love, prosperity, children, and grandchildren. They are also made aware of the curses of unfaithfulness or covenant-breaking.

The general concept of covenant is also practiced in real estate purchases. When one person agrees to purchase a house from someone else, both sign a legal document illustrating the authority of the civil government to enforce the contract. The purchaser is given an understanding of the terms of the agreement or the ethical requirements. For example, if he is delinquent with the mortgage payments, he risks losing the house to foreclosure; however, if he fulfills the agreement, he obtains the rights to the house and an inheritance for future generations.

Other examples of covenants in modern society can be seen when a professional athlete signs a contract with a team or when a person makes a vow to become an American citizen.

I personally made a covenant in my own life at the age of 19 when I gave my life to Christ. Although I didn't cut covenant by spilling my blood or by signing any legal documents in the presence of lawyers, it was a covenant nonetheless. On January 10, 1978, I confessed Christ as Lord over my life, acknowledging His transcendence. When I repented and promised that I would follow Him, I was in essence submitting to His ethical requirements.

As I continued to follow Christ, I understood that I would be filled with peace and joy and receive numerous answers to prayer when I obeyed His Word. But I also knew that I would sense His displeasure and experience discipline if I intentionally disobeyed (see Heb. 12:5-11). By continuing in His word, I am ensured of eternal life.

Broken Covenants

Having ministered in full-time church service for almost three decades, I have also witnessed the devastation that can come to an individual or a congregation when covenants are broken. One such story took place in the early days of our church.

A beautiful young lady in our congregation began to fall into very divisive behavior that involved, among other things, gossip, slander, and sexual immorality. After repeated warnings from fellow believers, she continued to participate in this behavior and eventually died of a terrible disease. As far as I know, she did repent and recommit her life to Christ while on her sickbed.

I remember another young man who precociously began to proclaim himself the prophetic mouthpiece of God to our congregation just a few short months after his conversion. We tried to admonish him, but unfortunately he chose not to listen to us and began to prophesy against us, pronouncing judgment on us for not receiving him as God's prophetic voice. I had no choice but to dis-fellowship him and warn him of God's judgment for allowing rebellion to come to his life. About three months later, we heard that he had died of an apparent suicide.

I have found that even congregations can break covenant with the Body of Christ. Not long ago, there was a church that was growing very rapidly here in the New York region. I found out that their members were encouraged to proselytize people from other evangelical churches, telling them that only this church would bring revival to our region. I felt a caution in my spirit, knowing that God was not pleased and would soon bring correction to their leadership. Sure enough, after less than five years of existence, sin was exposed in the eldership of the church. As a result, the pastor stepped down, they lost their facility, and their congregation fragmented into numerous smaller churches.

Yet another church sent letters to folks attending various evangelical churches that were struggling and told attendees that they would experience restoration and a closer walk with the Lord if they attended this new church. (Many leaders call this practice "fish swapping" because the "fish" are merely going from church to church.) When I met with this pastor, he told me that his church was experiencing true revival because they were feeding the people. I tried warning him that he was going to have problems because of stealing sheep. Within a few short years, they lost the large building they were meeting in and began experiencing an exodus of some of their top leaders. To his credit, this pastor wrote a letter of apology to the pastors in his community, admitting his wrongdoing and humbling himself.

A biblically successful church must be built on covenantal relationships. We should not simply leave our church if we are experiencing difficulty, just like we should not leave our husband or wife when tempted to divorce for objectionable reasons. We must learn to work out our differences, even getting help, if necessary, and we should love and honor each other by keeping covenant. Jesus, our ultimate model of covenant-keeping, still honored His covenant with His disciples even though some of them denied Him and all of them deserted Him when He was arrested and put on trial.

"In the Beginning"—The First Covenant

We must have a fuller understanding of biblical covenants so that we have a measuring stick or blueprint for how this can be manifested in our present lives.

God's first words to man were:

Be fruitful and increase in number; fill the earth and subdue it. Rule over the fish of the sea and the birds of the air and over every living creature that moves on the ground (Genesis 1:28 NIV).

Through this verse, we witness that God intended His Kingdom to be manifested on earth from the beginning of our earthly existence. This desire is mentioned many times in Scripture through His covenants with His people. Since God spoke about this time and time again, we can only assume that covenant is of great importance to Him.

Along these lines, there are those in the Church who believe that after the Fall of the human race, the Cultural Commission to have dominion over the earth was either nullified or put on hold until the physical return of Christ, when He will set up His earthly Kingdom. Yet all throughout the Bible, God defines the nature and mission of His covenant as being connected to the world around us.

From Genesis 2:15-17 on, every person God worked with made an agreement with Him to follow His law/word. The Old Testament major and minor prophets concentrated primarily on God's people and their covenants with Him. Malachi 3:5 illustrates that one of the primary roles of the prophets was to be covenant prosecutors. They spoke on God's behalf in an accusatory role when His people broke covenant with Him.

An amazing covenantal narrative unfolded when Adam and Eve disobeyed the first commandment that God gave them. They broke covenant and began the redemptive story that progressed through more covenants with those whom God found faithful. The original covenant was reconfirmed with Noah, given to Abraham, restated to Israel, and made again with David (see Gen. 9:1-3; 12:1-3; 17:5-7; Exod. 20; Deut. 28; 2 Sam. 7:16-17).

The New Testament reconfirms the original covenant through Jesus with the shedding of His blood (see Heb. 9:11-18; Matt. 26: 26-29; 28:18-20). Jesus inaugurated the new Kingdom Age in Mark 1:15, causing such a qualitative change in society that John described it as a new heaven and new earth.[3]

Its consummation is prophetically illustrated by the apostle John in Revelation 21:1-3. At that time, all the covenant promises will be fully reconciled due to the global influence of the Gospel in fulfillment of the Lord's Prayer in Luke 11:2: *"...Your kingdom come. Your will be done on earth as it is in heaven"* (NKJV).

The Bible is a covenant document to His covenant people because God doesn't do anything without a covenant. Jesus, acting as the representative of the human race (the second or last Adam), became the sacrificial lamb that reratified the original covenant with Adam (see 1 Cor. 15:45).

I believe that in order to have a comprehensive understanding of biblical context, we must understand that the Bible is unified by a continual ratification of the original covenant given to Adam.

The Five Points of the Biblical Covenant

In order to further explain covenant, I need to draw attention to the five-point covenantal structure that unlocks biblical interpretation. A biblical covenant involves transcendence, represen-tation, ethical stipulations, consequences for obedience or disobedience, and generational continuity.

Understanding this structure is important because it provides us with a blueprint for our relationships with God and others. This biblical insight will help us to serve Him and others better and will unlock why we may be falling short of manifesting the glory of God here on the earth (see Rom. 3:23).

God and His magnificence should be evident to the world through the testimony of the way we live our lives. Not only should we display model families and relationships and godly character, but we should also be far advanced in science and the arts. Christians should be the ones writing influential children's "God fiction" and excelling in athletics. Christians need to be the leading CEOs of the most promising and influential corporations, manifesting the glory of God in the business world as well.

King Solomon created such a spectacular kingdom that he was famous all throughout the ancient world. Other rulers feared and respected Israel because the glory of Solomon's God was unmistakable and far outshined their own futile existence. The Queen of Sheba was so overwhelmed with Solomon's wisdom and Israel's splendor that she said:

> *How happy your men must be! How happy your officials, who continually stand before you and hear your wisdom!* ***Praise be to the Lord your God, who has delighted in you and placed you on the throne of Israel...*** (1 Kings 10:8-9 NIV).

Yet despite our beautiful heritage of manifesting God's glory, today's American evangelical church has never had so much growth with so little impact on the culture. Statistically, there are more people attending church in America than ever before in our history, but our culture is moving progressively farther and farther from God's heart on issues such as legalized abortion, alternate forms of marriage, the incarceration of millions of people, and mass amounts of fraudulent subprime lending that is destroying the United States' economy.

Walking in all of the components of covenantal structure is vital for the Church if we are to experience the fullness of the Kingdom's blessings that will lead to cultural penetration and influence as Salt and Light (see Matt. 5:13-16).

1. *Transcendence*

The first component of biblical covenant is God's *transcendence,* which means that He is supreme and surpasses all others. In Scripture, God's transcendence is shown primarily in references regarding His role as creator and redeemer and in instances where He speaks directly to humanity.

When we discover the full requirements and implications of His transcendence, we will immediately see whether we have been treating God too casually or not seeking after Him as we would in a loving and respectful human relationship (see Prov. 9:10; Heb. 7:26). Answering two simple questions might give us a clue as to how we are currently living our lives:

1. Are we "searching out" to see God as He truly is?

2. Do we desire to know Him, His mysteries, and His divine wisdom?

In Genesis, we see God demonstrating His true transcendence as creator of the cosmos before He made a covenant with Adam and Eve (see Gen. 1:27-28; 2:15-17). Within Old Testament covenantal treaties, the suzerainty kings would first proclaim their own greatness before revealing the terms of the covenant. We see this principle illustrated in Exodus 20:2 when God identified Himself as the One who delivered Israel out of slavery, reminding His people of His power and preeminence over all the gods of Egypt.

This reminder of true transcendence was necessary since the nature of covenant involved full obedience on the part of the people in order for their great King to bless and protect them as they journeyed to and eventually entered the Promised Land.

We also witness a New Testament example of this in the Great Commission found in Matthew 28:18. Jesus claimed His true transcendence before He commissioned His disciples to go as His Kingdom representatives and disciple the nations by saying, *"All power is given unto Me in heaven and in earth."*

It is important for the Body of Christ to first have a vision of the greatness and sovereign power of our Creator God. Then we can have the faith and motivation to trust Him to keep His promise of protecting and granting eternal life when we willingly obey His covenant word.

2. Representatives

Covenant will also reveal the fact that we are called to *represent* Christ to the world as His delegated authority (see 2 Cor. 5:19-20; Matt. 28:19). Some believers think that salvation is only about their own fate in the afterlife. They forget that, while on earth, we have an obligation to others as God's stewards of the Gospel.

In Genesis 1:28, God called Adam as His representative to populate and, by implication, indoctrinate the earth with God's Kingdom principles. He said, *"...Subdue it: and have dominion over [it]...."* Thus, Adam was called to function as God's hierarchical representative of the whole human race, which of course resulted in a disaster when he fell into sin.[4]

Later, in Exodus 19:6 we see God calling Israel to be a nation of priests and to be His covenant representatives to all the nations of the world. It is important to note here, however, that this representation was conditional upon their ability to keep the ethical terms of His covenant. As long as they obeyed Him, representing His covenant to the nations, they would experience divine protection and have the power to create wealth (see Ps. 105:10-15; Deut. 8:18). This protection and power would confirm His covenant to the other nations of the world.

Just as Jesus was sent out by the Father to be His Kingdom representative, we also see Jesus sending His disciples out into the world as His ambassadors (see John 20:21). His Church was even given the judicial authority to determine who could function as a viable member of the Body of Christ (see Matt. 18:15-20; John 20:23) and to manifest His plan and purpose to the rest of the visible and invisible cosmos (see Matt. 13:11; Eph. 1:9; 3:9-11).

As you can see, becoming a part of the Body of Christ carries with it the most amazing privilege coupled with the most awesome responsibility. As His representatives, we will even be called to judge angelic beings (see 1 Cor. 6:1-3).

3. Ethical Stipulations

The third aspect is the *ethical stipulations* or requirements of the covenant. We have been given thousands of commands to obey in order to live out our Christian lives, such Galatians 5:16-26 and Ephesians 5:1–6:9. This whole concept goes against our current postmodern, wishy-washy evangelical climate in which we have turned the Ten Commandments into the ten suggestions for a better life. Ethical stipulations are necessary because there are always certain behaviors that the King expects from those who pledge to serve Him in return for His protection.

The first instance of this is shown in Genesis 2:17 when God told Adam and Eve not to eat of the fruit of the Tree of the Knowledge of Good and Evil as a requirement for continuing to experience the blessings of His presence in the Garden of Eden.

We also see how God followed this covenantal principle with Israel when, after delivering them from Egypt and making them His covenant people, He gave them the Ten Commandments and civic laws so they could remain in good standing with Him (see Exod. 20–23).

In the New Testament, after describing His true transcendence over heaven and earth, Jesus instructs His disciples to teach the commandments of the covenant to the nations (see Matt. 28:20). Matthew 5:17-19 teaches us that Jesus continued the ethical stipulations of the Old Testament covenant law and demanded that all His disciples follow these covenantal commandments (see John 13:34; 14:15).

An example of this is when Jesus forgave the woman taken in adultery and then told her to *"go and sin no more"* (John 8:11). This shows that Jesus was not only acting as her Savior but also as her Lord and Master. Many people want Jesus to be their Savior, but He must first be their Lord. Romans 10:9 clearly explains that we must first confess Christ as Lord before experiencing biblical salvation. Lordship and ethical commands go hand in hand.

4. Sanctions

The fourth aspect of the covenant has to do with *sanctions* or the consequences of obedience and disobedience to the ethical requirements of the covenant. A large percentage of believers have the false notion that God is merely a dispenser of blessings. They believe that there are no consequences for sin because we are no longer held by the works of the law but justified by grace through faith.

Paul had something very interesting to say about this in Romans 6:1-2: *"What shall we say, then? Shall we go on sinning so that grace may increase? By no means! We died to sin; how can we live in it any longer?"* (NIV).

Jude 4 says that some people falsely believe that the grace of God is a license to live in sin. Consequently, America is inundated with positive self-help messages with no mention of repentance, hell, and the judgment that comes for failing to adhere to God's sanctions.

In my many years of experience, I have witnessed hundreds of believers simultaneously experience both the forgiveness of *and* the consequences for their sin. In particular, I have seen God forgive the sin of adultery but not exclude that person from having to deal with the enormous repercussions of broken covenants.

In Genesis 2:17 we see the first instance of sanctions when God warned Adam that the day he ate of the fruit of the Tree of the Knowledge of Good and Evil, he would die. This was fulfilled when he and Eve ate of the forbidden fruit and were subsequently dismissed from the presence of the Lord in the Garden of Eden (see Gen. 3:24).

In Deuteronomy 28:15-68 we find a detailed explanation of the consequences that Israel would experience if they broke covenant with God and forsook His ethical stipulations. Every kind of evil would be unleashed on the disobedient, including every sickness and disease known and unknown, every kind of mental and emotional problem, financial troubles, barrenness of the womb, and the captivity of their wives and children who would become the spoils taken in war.

In the past 50 years, our generation has seen firsthand how broken covenants have negatively impacted our culture. With the national divorce rate hovering above 50 percent, fragmented families are seeing their children reap the devastating results of these broken covenants.

Numerous statistics show that a committed marriage between one man and one woman is essential for the physical, emotional, mental, and economic health of children.[5] Professor of law Robin Fretwell Wilson wrote an article in which she encourages the state to support marriage; because by supporting marriage, they are supporting children.[6]

My wife Joyce felt the need to found an organization called Children of the City to reach these at-risk young victims of divorce and broken covenants. Our three decades of ministry and public service have shown us that there is a direct correlation between the lack of a fatherly presence and a child's gang and drug involvement. These children often fail to complete high school, lack work ethics, and are eventually incarcerated because they lack the guidance of a two-parent family.

Many, if not most, of the children in our neighborhood are being raised primarily by their mothers due to divorce or lack of marital commitment on the part of the father. As good as a mother may be, she can never take the place of a loving and involved father (just as a father can never take the place of a mother).

Both boys and girls are negatively affected by fatherlessness. Girls in particular, when there is no father in their life, often seek to fill that absence of fatherly affection in some other way, sometimes by getting involved romantically with older men or boys and experiencing teen pregnancy.

God warned us in Malachi concerning the consequences of broken family covenants. In fact, Malachi 4:6 says that unless the hearts of the fathers are turned toward the children and the children toward the fathers, God is going to strike the earth with a curse.

The problem is that our modern mentality creates room for relativism or excuses for our actions, thereby absolving us of personal responsibility for sin and broken covenants. Even though we are redeemed from the curse of the law at the moment of our conversion (see Gal. 3:13), we are not absolved of the consequences of our disobedience. Jesus told the man He healed at the pool of Bethesda in John 5:14 to *"stop sinning or something worse may happen to you"* (NIV).[7]

The apostle Paul told the Corinthian church to hand over the person who was having an affair with his father's wife to satan "for the destruction of the flesh" (1 Cor. 5:5). He told the Galatian church that in sowing to their fleshly desires they would reap the judgment that comes from breaking the covenant (see Gal. 6:7-8). And he told the church in Ephesus that the "wrath of God" would come upon the "children of disobedience" (Eph. 5:6).

Of course, the ultimate consequence for not keeping God's covenant is eternal damnation, which Jesus warned us of in Matthew 10:28 (see also John 3:16-19). Those in the Church who think the New Testament is a lawless dispensation with no consequences for covenant breakers should conduct a careful search of the Scriptures. When Jesus inaugurated the New Covenant, He progressively built upon, rather than negating, all of the earlier covenants (see Matt. 5:17-20).

I personally believe that those chosen by God will ultimately persevere in their faith because they are kept by Jesus (see John 17:11-12; Jude 1, 24) and are predestined for salvation (see Acts 13:48; Eph. 1:4; Rom. 8:28-30). Yet Scripture does admonish us to continue in the faith lest we believed in vain; because if we fall away we demonstrate that we were never a part of Christ to begin with (see 1 Cor. 15:1-2; Col. 1:22-23; Heb. 3:13-15; 1 John 2:19)!

5. Continuity

Last but not least, Christians who discover the true meaning of covenant will see that God expects all believers to serve Him with *continuity* or a plan for multiple generations. Because knowledge of covenant is virtually nonexistent in today's Church, we don't often think in terms of continuity. In our postmodern mentality, we make decisions based on what we see and what we desire at the moment. However, every time a major decision in life is made regarding family, church, ministry, business, or community, we should be conscious of how it will affect the generations to come.

One of the greatest downfalls of focusing on the traditional views of the Rapture and the imminent return of the Lord is that believers are diverted from having a multigenerational plan. Thus, some have asked, "Why get involved in education, save money, or invest for the future if the world is going to end soon?"

A careful study of the Scriptures reveals that God will only transfer the wealth of the sinner to the righteous if they have a financial plan for at least three generations (see Prov. 13:22). Those who plan for multiple generations will be the ones to gain access to all that is needed for attaining true dominion over the earth.

It is vital to note that because of their belief system regarding having large families, Muslims plan to set up Muslim Emirates that will have dominion in Western Europe within 50 years. Europeans, the original occupiers of the land, are dying faster than they are reproducing. By 2050, it is quite possible that Islam will be the dominant religion and possibly even the dominant culture in France, Italy, Spain, and England.

This is a subtle plan of the enemy to copy aspects of the original covenant to bear fruit and multiply and to gain dominion on the earth. The Muslim faith is rapidly spreading because its adherents believe in and obey the original Cultural Commission more than the present-day Christian Church does!

One powerful biblical illustration of planning for multiple generations is found in the lineage of King David. Genesis 38 teaches us that Judah and his daughter-in-law Tamar had an illegitimate child, breaking a particular law of the covenant found in Deuteronomy 23:2. Heirs of an illegitimate son could not enter into the tabernacle of the Lord for at least ten generations.

David was born exactly ten generations after Judah and Tamar's son, Perez. That means that the tribe of Judah had to disciple and keep their children in the faith without a leader in the assembly of the Lord for a very long period of time. They were able to do this because their obedience to the covenant involved a multigenerational approach, which is a far cry from the present one-generational, Rapture-frenzied mindset of many evangelical churches.

In the New Testament we see this principle expressed in Peter's message to the people on the Day of Pentecost. He told the crowd that this promise he was speaking about was for them, their children, and their children's children (see Acts 2:39).

I believe that we will not begin to understand the full Gospel until we rediscover the fullness of the biblical covenant. All in all, the rediscovery of covenant has the potential to be a culturally transformative cataclysm!

It will be like the days when Israel's King Josiah read the words of the covenant for the first time and realized that the idols, Asherah poles, and altars to other gods were detrimental to God's people. His reforms and humility resulted in a revival of faith for the whole nation, and it was said that his Passover feast was the greatest since the days of the prophet Samuel (see 2 Chron. 34:19-33).

My prayer is that when the power of covenant is rediscovered, the Body of Christ will be reformed in the same way that Israel was under King Josiah. Covenantal continuity is so important to God that He identified Himself to His people in terms of a tri-generational relationship with the patriarchs of Israel. He called Himself the God of Abraham, Isaac, and Jacob.

THINK ON THIS

Our salvation is a wonderful gift that not only saves us individually, but should also bring about great reform in our neighborhoods and communities. God takes this covenantal relationship with Him very seriously and through it admonishes and empowers us to bring about the cultural change to our world that will reflect His Kingdom principles.

Review each of the components of God's covenant, and see what you need to do in pursuit of your personal, God-given cultural commission.

1. *Transcendence:* When we discover the full requirements and implications of His transcendence, we will immediately know whether we have been treating God too casually or not seeking after Him as we would in a loving and respectful human relationship (see Prov. 9:10; Heb. 7:26). Answering two simple questions will give you a clue as to how you are currently living your life in regards to this component of covenant:

   Are you "searching out" to see God as He truly is?

Do you desire to know Him, His mysteries, and His divine wisdom?

If your answers are "yes," then what would you do with this information to fulfill your Cultural Commission once you found it?

2. *Representatives:* As believers, we are also called to represent Christ to the world as His delegated authority (see 2 Cor. 5:19-20; Matt. 28:19). In Genesis 1:28, God called Adam as His representative to populate and, by implication, indoctrinate the earth with God's Kingdom principles.

   Explain how God's commission to subdue the earth and have dominion over it applies to your life.

   Becoming part of the Body of Christ carries with it the most amazing privilege and a most awesome responsibility. List some responsibilities you personally have as God's representative:

   At your job:

   In your home:

   In your neighborhood:

   In your local church:

3. *Ethical Stipulations:* These are the commands we have been given to obey throughout our Christian lives. Read and explain the two examples given in this chapter:

   a. Galatians 5:16-26

   b. Ephesians 5:1-6:9

   Why are ethical stipulations necessary in our lives?

4. *Sanctions:* These are the consequences of obedience and disobedience to the ethical requirements of the covenant. Read Romans 6:1-7; then answer "yes" or "no" to the following questions concerning sanctions.

   Is God merely a dispenser of blessings to Christians?

Are there consequences for sin even though we are no longer held by the works of the law but are justified by grace through faith?

Shall we go on sinning so that grace may increase?

5. *Continuity:* God expects all believers to serve Him with a plan for multiple generations. Complete the following mind-set that we must begin to live by if we desire to fully walk in the benefits of God's covenant with us:

Every time a major decision in life is made regarding family, church, ministry, business, or community, we should be...

Endnotes

1. This is a true story taken from the testimony of a missionary to Mexico.

2. Due to the Fall, Abraham couldn't walk between the pieces because the righteousness of his seed could not be of himself. Christ alone could be the righteous seed of Abraham to fulfill this covenant (see Gal. 3:15-25; Rom. 3:12; 2 Cor. 5:21). Hebrews 6:13-20 adds colorful commentary to this episode.

3. Second Peter 3:13 calls this new heaven and new earth the *"home of righteousness."*

4. Read the results of the Fall in Romans 5:12-19.

5. Elizabeth Marquardt, *Between Two Worlds: The Inner Lives of Children of Divorce* (New York: Crown Publishing Group, 2005).

6. Robin Fretwell Wilson, http://www.law.umaryland.edu/faculty_publications.a sp?facultynum=280

7. See also the sicknesses that the curse of the law unleashes in Deuteronomy 28:58-61.

CHAPTER 4

COVENANT AND THE
CULTURAL COMMISSION

*Therefore go and make disciples of **all** nations, baptizing them in the name of the Father and of the Son and of the Holy Spirit, and teaching them to obey **everything** I have commanded you* (Matthew 28:19 NIV).

Often the five points of covenantal structure that we discussed in the previous chapter are demonstrated when the Lord reveals Himself to someone and commissions them for service. This chapter will illustrate how the five points of covenant unite to reinforce the Cultural Commission of Genesis 1:28 and give us a clearer understanding of God's purpose for His people throughout history. When we understand this, we can begin to more effectively fulfill the Great Commission that Jesus has given us as His representatives on the earth today.

Covenant With Adam

Read Genesis 2:15-18.

The Five Components

Transcendence: God took Adam and put him in the Garden of Eden.

Representatives: God set Adam in the Garden to dress and keep it; therefore, man was commissioned for service unto God.

Ethical Stipulations: God told Adam which trees to eat from and which were forbidden.

Sanctions: God told Adam that the consequence of eating the forbidden fruit was death.

Continuity: God provided Eve as Adam's helper for continuity of the human race.

As we study the Scriptures, we will see how the first covenant with Adam holds the key to understanding all other major themes of the Bible.

Covenant With Noah

Read Genesis 9:1-2,5-7,9.

The Five Components

Transcendence: God, as judge, revealed Himself as He blessed and spoke to Noah.

Representatives: God chose Noah as the new federal head to represent Him and replenish the earth.

Ethical Stipulations: God commanded Noah to be fruitful and multiply.

Sanctions: Sanctions were pronounced on those who shed the blood of other human beings.

Continuity: God spoke to Noah and his family and told them that they would bring forth abundantly and multiply and that God would establish His covenant with them and their seed after them.

The Cultural Commission

The Noahic Covenant is a restating of Adam's Cultural Commission. After the earth was baptized (judged) by the flood of waters, God placed Noah as the new federal head of the re-created earth. Through him, God would continue His covenantal relationship with the human race.

Covenant With Abram/Abraham

Read Genesis 12:1-3,7.

The Five Components

Transcendence: Jehovah revealed Himself to Abram and spoke to him.

Representatives: God chose Abram to inherit the land of promise.

Ethical Stipulations: God commanded Abram to leave his country and family and go to the land He would show him.

Sanctions: God said He would bless Abram for obeying Him and curse those who cursed him.

Continuity: God promised Abram that in him all the families of the earth would be blessed and that God was going to give his seed the land.

The Cultural Commission

Since God used Noah to begin the human race anew, the Cultural Commission was repeated almost verbatim to him. With Abram (Abraham), God was able to develop this covenant further and to deal with it in more detail.[1]

Although the language used in Abraham's covenant is different from that used in Genesis 1:28, the goal is the same: All of the families of the earth will be blessed in Abraham. In other words, the blessing of God's covenant is not to stay with one family or people group, but is to eventually reach into every tribe and tongue so that every family of the earth receives a blessing from God. Because blessings come from obedience, this implies that every nation and ethnic group will be given the word of God and discipled by the chosen seed of Abraham.

Further Explication

Read Genesis 17:1-7.

In this passage God's words are more specific. He tells Abraham that nations and kings will come out of his loins. This addresses other aspects of Genesis 1:28, which tells God's people to be fruitful and multiply and to have dominion. That is to say, the seed of Abraham is to exercise great influence on the political, social, economic, and religious lives of whole nations.[2] In the New Testament, the apostle Paul also said that the seed of Abraham is the Church (see Gal. 3:29).

The Abrahamic Covenant Continued

Read Genesis 22:17-18.

In this passage, God again uses the terms *blessing* and *multiplying* and then states that Abraham's *"seed shall possess the gate of his enemies."* Since *gate* in the Old Testament refers to the place where the elders of a city ruled and made decisions regarding economics, politics, war, real estate, and judicial matters, it is commonly accepted that the gates represent the political power of a city or nation (see Prov. 31:23).

Today our "gate" is the place where the mayor and city legislators make decisions and conduct business. For example, our national gate would be the White House. Although spoken differently, this passage demonstrates a powerful continuation of the Cultural Commission in Genesis 1:28, especially in regard to subduing our enemies and having dominion in the nations of the earth.[3]

In modern times, we can say that the words *subduing* and *having dominion* indicate God's call for His covenant law and people to *replace* current leaders in every realm of society including education, law, economics, politics, heath, philosophy, science, art, music, theater, and sports. Thus, the laws of the covenant can break down the ungodly systems that are currently controlling our nation's political, economic, and sociological structures and replace them with God's Kingdom culture.

God wants His covenantal people and laws to have dominion on the earth because sin is not just imbedded in individual human beings; it is also systemic. If we are going to experience lasting positive change in the earth, we not only need more Christians involved in those areas, but we also need Christian *ways* of doing them.

The Abrahamic Covenant is continued again in Genesis 26:4-6 and 28:14-15 where God repeats the covenant of multiplication and blessing to all the nations of the earth through Abraham's son, Isaac, and his grandson, Jacob.

Covenant With Moses

Read Exodus 3:1-22.

The Five Components[4]

Transcendence: God was revealed to Moses in the burning bush.

Representatives: Moses was commissioned to speak and act for God to Pharaoh.

Ethical Stipulations: God commanded Moses to release Israel from captivity. The ethical stipulations were both for Moses in regards to him obeying the command and for Pharaoh in regards to releasing the children of Israel from captivity.

Sanctions: God said that He would smite Egypt with punishment for not obeying His command.

Continuity: The Egyptians would provide the sustenance for the Jews leaving captivity.

The Cultural Commission

Read Deuteronomy 28:1-13.

The message of dominion and blessing could not be stronger here. The language of Genesis 1:28 is echoed this time through Moses to the nation of Israel.[5]

Covenant With King David

Read Second Samuel 7:1-17.

The Five Components

Transcendence: God spoke to David through Nathan the prophet, saying, *"Thus saith the Lord."*

Representatives: God said that He took David from shepherding sheep to shepherding His people.

Ethical Stipulations: God commanded David to be the ruler over Israel and to take the place of the Judges.

Sanctions: God said that He cut off (judged) all of David's enemies and blessed him by making his name great.

Continuity: God told David that He would plant the children of Israel. He also told David that He would set up his seed after him and establish his kingdom forever.

The Cultural Commission

God continues to perpetuate the Cultural Commission through David by promising him that his seed will establish a Kingdom that will last forever. The closer we get to Christ, the more specific the promises get, but all of them echo the context of the Cultural Commission: dominion, blessing, and multiplication of seed.

Covenant Through Jesus

Read Matthew 28:16-20.

The Five Components

Transcendence: Jesus appeared to the disciples on the mountain.

Representatives: Jesus said that all power was delegated to Him.

Ethical Stipulations: Jesus commanded His disciples to baptize nations.

Sanctions: Jesus told His disciples to give the nations commandments, implying blessing for obedience and cursing for disobedience.

Continuity: Jesus ensured His disciples that He would be with them always, even unto the end of the world.

The Cultural Commission

The Great Commission passage in Matthew is the New Testament equivalent of Genesis 1:28, in which Jesus, as the last Adam (see 1 Cor. 15:45), is recommissioning His covenant people to complete the work that the first Adam and Israel failed to do. Without this interpretation, the covenants are disconnected and do not cohere. This also connects Christ to the cosmological call that Adam had as God's vice-regent to disciple the nations and exercise dominion over the created order.

The New Testament Church: The Corinthians

Read First Corinthians 1.

The Five Components

Transcendence: Paul blesses the church from *"God our Father, and from the Lord Jesus Christ"* (1 Cor. 1:3).

Representatives: Paul said that the grace of God was given to them in Christ Jesus (see 1 Cor. 1:4).

Ethical Stipulations: Paul admonished the church to walk in unity (see 1 Cor. 1:10).

Sanctions: God said that He would "destroy the wisdom of the wise" (1 Cor. 1:19-20).

Continuity: God said He would "save those who believe" (1 Cor. 1:21 NKJV).

This passage in First Corinthians implies that God is going to use the Church to ideologically dismantle the false philosophical systems of ungodly culture and demonstrate the ascendancy of the Gospel of the Kingdom.

The New Testament Church: The Ephesians

Read Revelation 2:1-7.

The Five Components

Transcendence: Jesus revealed Himself as *"He that holdeth the seven stars in His right hand,"* and *"who walketh in the midst of the seven golden candlesticks"* (Rev. 2:1).

Representatives: Jesus commends the church for representing His Kingdom by testing those who say they are apostles (see Rev. 2:2).

Ethical Stipulations: Jesus commands the church to *"repent, and do the first works"* (Rev. 2:5).

Sanctions: Jesus warned them that if they did not repent, He would come quickly and remove their candlestick (see Rev. 2:5).

Continuity: Jesus promises that overcomers will *"eat of the tree of life, which is in the midst of the paradise of God"* (Rev. 2:7).

This teaches that overcomers can presently experience a taste of God's Kingdom on earth as it was meant to be before the Fall—thus fulfilling the Lord's Prayer, "Thy kingdom come, Thy will be done on earth as it is in heaven."

The Cultural Commission

Having made known unto us the mystery of His will, according to His good pleasure which He hath purposed in Himself: that in the dispensation of the fullness of times He might gather together in one all things in Christ, both which are in heaven, and which are on earth; even in Him: in whom also we have obtained an inheritance, being predestinated according to the purpose of Him who worketh all things after the counsel of His own will (Ephesians 1:9-11).

Regarding the victory of Christ that reconciled both the cosmos and the human race back to Him, Paul tells the Church that the supreme mystery of God has now been revealed. According to Paul, God desires all things to be under His lordship.

This should be the mission of the Church—not just to win individual souls, but to claim every aspect of culture and life for God. Ephesians 4:10 says that Christ rose from the dead to *"fill all things."* Ephesians 1:22-23 tells us that the Church is the primary instrument He has commissioned to *"put all things under His feet"* and to "[fill] *all in all."*[6]

Culmination of the Cultural Commission

*And I saw a **new** heaven and a **new** earth: for the first heaven and the first earth were passed away; and there was no more sea. And I John saw the holy city, **new** Jerusalem, coming down from God out of heaven, prepared as a bride adorned for her husband. And I heard a great voice out of heaven saying, Behold, the tabernacle of God is with men, and He will* *dwell with them, and they shall be His people, and God Him-self shall be with them, and be their God* (Revelation 21:1-3).

The culmination of life as shown in the Book of Revelation is when a new heaven and a new earth appear. The Greek word for "new" used here is *kainos,* which means "qualitatively new, fresh, unworn." This is in contrast to the Greek word *neos,* which refers to numerically new, or new in relation to time, young, or recent.[7] This use of the word *kainos* rather than *neos* strongly implies that the passage is speaking more about drastic quality of life changes (societal transformation) rather than a whole new heaven and earth.

How this happens is explained in verse 2, in which the apostle John says he saw the New Jerusalem *"coming down from God out of heaven."* That is to say, John saw the uniting of heaven and earth, or the influence of the Kingdom of God on earth throughout history as the Gospel of the Kingdom goes forth.

This also helps us understand what Revelation 19:11-16 means when the Church is described as going forth behind Christ as our King to spread His Kingdom influence on the earth. The culmination of this would then be a *"new heaven and new earth."* And that comports with the ultimate goal of believers having dominion in the created order as found originally in Genesis 1:28.

Although this is only a brief overview of Scripture from Genesis to Revelation, we can easily see that the Cultural Commission found in Genesis 1:28 is the key to connecting all other covenants. This lays the foundation for the rest of the covenants and helps us to interpret Scripture.

Because these covenants reveal the purpose of creation, they give us a greater understanding of how we should be living out our faith. Those who grasp the fullness of the biblical covenant will be forever transformed and come into a greater relationship with God that involves not only saying a so-called "sinner's prayer" and attending church once a week, but a covenantal way of life. It will enable a transcendent view of God in which we are called to be His representatives on the earth who will both obey and apply the demands of His covenant for generations to come.

A Reflection of Him

Those who walk in biblical covenant actually mimic the Godhead because even the Father, Son, and Holy Spirit function together in covenant. When Jesus made a covenant with His disciples at the Last Supper (see Matt. 26:26-28), He was acting out the agreement He had already made with the Father and the Holy Spirit in eternity. Revelation 13:8 states that Jesus was slain by covenantal agreement from before the foundation of the world.

Furthermore, sometime after His incarnation but before His crucifixion, Jesus quoted parts of Psalm 40, which talks about an eternal agreement He had made to take on a human body so He could be a sacrifice for sins. This was reiterated in Hebrews 10:5: *"Therefore, when Christ came into the world, He said, 'Sacrifice and offering You did not desire, but a body You prepared for Me'"* (NIV).

It is only when the Church understands and walks in the various components of biblical covenant that we will be able to fully exert God's Kingdom influence in every realm of life.

THINK ON THIS

As we conclude this chapter, it is worth pausing to think about how the Cultural Commission affects the way we view our Christian calling to influence cities and nations for Jesus.

Write out in your own words what living a biblical covenantal life means to you personally.

Using the five point covenantal structure, find other passages that fit this structure.

Try to remember the key people and covenants God used from Genesis to Revelation to continue the Cultural Commission of Genesis 1:28.

Explain why the "Great Commission" in Matthew 28:19-20 is the New Testament equivalent of the "Cultural Commission" in Genesis 1:28.

In light of this chapter, how do you now view the culmination of the Cultural Commission as taught in Revelation 21:1-3?

Endnotes

1. The covenant with Adam wasn't originally as complex because the human race was sinless at the time. After the Fall, the Cultural Commission had to gradually be unpacked so that the Second Adam, Jesus Christ, could come through a specific people who were in covenant with Him.

2. Some say that in the term *kings* God was simply predicting that Israel would have kings, but they miss that the context here is not just Israel. In verse 6 it tells us that this is referring to the plural *nations,* not to the one nation Israel.

3. While the majority of the people in the Church today are happy when a political leader gives them a place at the table, this passage tells us that we should be the ones who set the table and lead the discussion.

4. For a more in-depth study on the five-point biblical covenant, read Ray Sutton's book, *That You May Prosper.*

5. The promises of being above, not beneath, of lending to many nations, and of not borrowing were not given to the whole world, but only to those who walked in covenant with God. This is in opposition to those who hold that the Cultural Commission in Genesis 9:1-2 was given to the whole world and not just to God's people through Noah.

6. Ephesians 4:11-12 states that God gives certain individuals gifts to prepare the Church for the work of the ministry. According to verse 10, that is to *"fill all things."* Those who espouse the Cultural Commission believe that God has called the Church to infiltrate every domain of life and claim them for the glory of God. The preparing of God's people for the work of the ministry must include releasing Christians in every walk of life to subdue the earth and have dominion in all facets of society. Galatians 4:7 and Romans 4:13 speak about the seed of Abraham being heirs of God and inheriting the world. We are not called to escape the earth but to explore, enjoy, and subdue it for the glory of God.

7. *Blue Letter Bible,* "Dictionary and Word Search for *kainos (Strong's 2537)* and *neos (Strong's 3501)*." *Blue Letter Bible.* 1996-2009. Accessed May 10, 2009, on the Internet at http://www.blueletterbible.org.

CHAPTER 5
THE KING OF THE KINGDOM

*And Jesus came up and spoke to them, saying, "**All authority has been given to Me in heaven and on earth. Go therefore and make disciples of all the nations,** baptizing them in the name of the Father and the Son and the Holy Spirit, teaching them to observe all that I commanded you; and lo, I am with you always, even to the end of the age"* (Matthew 28:18-20 NASB).

In this great Cultural Commission to His disciples, Jesus clearly stated that He has been given the authority to rule God's Kingdom and has delegated certain responsibilities to us as members of His Kingdom. We will never truly understand the Kingdom of God and our role as His representatives without understanding the role of Jesus as its King.

We can't separate the person of Christ from His call as a King. Psalms 2 and 110 define Christ's royal position as ruler over the nations as the Only Lord and Potentate. This chapter will prove that Jesus is the undisputed King of kings and Lord of lords. And this fact is vital to the Cultural Commission because it means that Jesus holds all earthly rulers responsible for how they govern their nations, cities, and communities—thus making cultural involvement a stewardship issue for all believers.

Also, we will see that, as King, Jesus is not just dwelling in Heaven, distant and uninvolved with His creation. And we will see later on in this chapter how the phrase "Kingdom of God" seems to imply His rule over the whole universe (or cosmos), whereas the "Kingdom of Heaven" seems to imply the personal place of His dwelling.

King of Kings

In John 18:37, Pilate asked Jesus if He was a king:

...Jesus answered, "You say correctly that I am a king. For this I have been born, and for this I have come into the world, to testify to the truth. Everyone who is of the truth hears My voice" (NASB).

Earlier in John 10, Jesus said that those who were truly His followers listened to Him and understood that He was sent by God to establish a new cultural order.

Jesus challenged the status quo in both religion and society with His teaching and His life. Though it is impossible to compare anyone to Christ, both Martin Luther, who radically changed both church and world history by initiating the Protestant Reformation, and Martin Luther King Jr., who caused a huge cultural shift by challenging the status quo in the area of racism, certainly exemplify working to bring God's Kingdom principles from Heaven to impact the earthly realm.

Jesus not only challenged the status quo, but He boldly declared Himself to be the King of kings. Imagine if Jesus were walking the earth today, followed by cameras from every news organization as He reiterates that He is the President of all presidents. He bases His authority to do this on Scriptures like Psalm 2 and 110 where God declares that He has personally installed Jesus as King of kings. He boldly declares that He is setting up a new Kingdom based exclusively on God's principles, which will eventually replace all the current forms of government. Traveling around the world, Jesus attracts crowds numbering in the multiple thousands as He holds public meetings to teach and explain God's Kingdom principles. His followers are so dedicated to Him that they are willing to advocate for change with Him and are even willing to die for Him. They begin to plan a spiritual, ideological, and cultural shift that will transform the gates (political power and systems) of the White House and every other place of power in the world.

Although that example may be difficult to swallow, it submits a contemporary picture of how revolutionary Jesus was in His day. This hypothetical scenario would most likely result in the execution of Jesus just as it did 2,000 years ago because of the political fear He would strike into the hearts of the powers that be.

Choose This Day

The Jewish leaders rejected Jesus 2,000 years ago because His rule spelled the end of their religious and economic dominance over Israel. Matthew 2:2-3 illustrates how the earthly King Herod and all his political leaders were troubled when Jesus was born because He was proclaimed King.

Both John 19:12-15 and Acts 17:5-8 show that the primary reason Jesus was crucified was for political not spiritual reasons. The Jewish people and their leaders chose an earthly king over the heavenly King just as they did in the days of the Prophet Samuel when they asked God for an earthly king to lead them (see 1 Sam. 8:4-9). There is no such thing as neutrality; the rejection of Christ meant their acquiescence to the Roman Caesar as the head of Israel.

We must truly understand why Jesus was crucified so that we realize the importance of our involvement in the political and social structures of our world. I used to think Jesus was crucified and the early Church was persecuted because they advocated a new religion. The truth of the matter is that Roman culture was imbued with polytheism, the worship of many gods. The Romans didn't care that another religion was beginning. They crucified Jesus and persecuted the early Church because Jesus' followers believed Him when He declared Himself the King over all the rulers of the earth.

The Sanhedrin wanted Jesus dead because He threatened their power base. When Pilate sought to release Jesus, the Jews knew what to say to provoke Pilate and get Jesus killed: *"Whoever makes himself a king speaks against Caesar"* (John 19:12 NKJV).

Caesar or Christ

The choice between Caesar and Christ is still before us today. Culture can either be ruled by the vicissitudes of men or by the immutable law (word) of God. When Jesus rose from the dead, He was given the title and name *"King of kings and Lord of lords"* (Rev. 19:16). This means that He is now the Boss of all bosses, President of all presidents, and Prime Minister of all prime ministers in this world, not just the Head of the Church. Paul said in Ephesians 1:17-23 that Jesus was given a name that is *above all* names, both in this world and that which is to come.

Consequently, what a nation does in regards to health care, immigration, poverty, the environment, economics, politics, education, and science is as much the concern of Jesus as what goes on in the Church. Every president, prime minister, mayor, and federal, state, and local elected official is accountable to Jesus as their Boss, irrespective of whether or not he or she is a Christian.

It is up to the Church to leverage her influence and promote governments and social systems that please the Lord Jesus by reflecting biblical principles. I believe in the separation of church and state, but not the separation of God and state.

As explained in a previous chapter, the Church sphere is only one of the five main spheres (jurisdictions) in God's Kingdom. Although the state and society are not primarily ecclesial, they are still under the overarching domain of God's Kingdom rule. Therefore the influence of God and state should never be separated.

We all have a choice of whether to submit to the government of God or the government of man. First Samuel 8:10-18 tells us the sort of things that will happen if we choose a human government that does not submit to Jesus as King. This passage is still applicable to us today, so carefully consider the consequences presented here for allowing the state to rule outside the precepts of Scripture.

1. Our children will possibly fight unjust wars to fulfill the desires of the state and king (see 1 Sam. 8:11-12).

2. Our children will be groomed vocationally to serve for the pleasures of the state and king (see 1 Sam. 8:13).

3. The king will take the best of our fields and vineyards for his own pleasure (see 1 Sam. 8:14). This is now called eminent domain, which is when the civic government claims the legal right to take property from private homeowners and or businesses for the supposed economic good of the state or community.

4. The king will extract at least 10 percent to support the state (see 1 Sam. 8:15-17). God frowns upon any state extracting a financial amount equal to or more than the tithe that He requires for worship. States that take more than 10 percent of the income from its citizens in taxes set themselves up above God as the savior and provider of the people.

Of course, many of these "consequences" are the norm in today's culture. For example, most Americans don't realize that before 1913, residents of the United States didn't have to pay income tax. Amendment XVI was passed by Congress on July 2, 1909, and ratified February 3, 1913, saying, "The Congress shall have power to lay and collect taxes on incomes, from whatever source derived, without apportionment among the several States, and without regard to any census or enumeration."

This initial income tax rate was set at only 1 percent of annual income. What a far cry that is from today, where the average United States citizen gives about 30 percent of his or her income to "Uncle Sam." And that does not even include the additional taxes levied on marriage, any local sales tax, and the inheritance tax, which robs our children of half the assets we want to leave them, even though this money has already been taxed. (As high as our taxes are, the countries of Western Europe—France and Italy, for example—have a much higher tax rate!)

When all is said and done, average United States citizens are taxed more than 50 percent of their income. Double taxation is not only wrong, but it is also an example of the oppression and proclivity toward central monetary control that people with a socialistic worldview exhibit. Do we really want to choose Caesar over Jesus?

Of course, the average citizen cannot immediately do anything about this on their own, but the Church needs to engage in a long-term process of training and electing leaders who will have monetary and political values (Kingdom values) that give more freedom to individuals to control their own wealth.

No Doubt

When Jesus came, He didn't hide the fact that He was coming as a King to start a cultural and religious revolution. The following passages clearly reveal that His purpose was to eternally reign as King of kings:

1. He announced the arrival of a Kingdom. Jesus told the people, *"Repent: for the kingdom of Heaven is at hand"* in Matthew 4:17. (See also Mark 1:15.)

2. He called Himself a King in John 18:37.

3. He called His followers the *ekklesia* in Matthew 16:18. *Ekklesia* is the Greek word for church. In the Greco-Roman culture, citizens formed an ekklesia when they assembled together to enact public policy and, in effect, function like a congress or parliament. This is the most politically charged word Jesus could have used to describe His followers.

4. He called His ekklesia to assault the gates of hell in Matthew 16:18. (Remember that Proverbs 31:23 tells us that the gates were the places of power, where the elders of a city made decisions.)

Of course, the major difference between Jesus' approach and Islam's call for a holy war is the fact that Jesus and the New Testament apostles never advocate forced conversions or spreading the Gospel with the sword. As a matter of fact, the apostle Paul said in Ephesians 6:10-12 that our struggle is not against flesh and blood. During the first 300 years of the Church, most Christians wouldn't even fight as a soldier in a war. The early Church of the first four centuries never shed blood in defense of the faith.

Revelation 19:16 and First Timothy 6:15 call Jesus the King of kings and Lord of lords. These verses connect Christ, His Kingdom, and His Church with the cultural mandate in Genesis 1:28 and subsequently with this world's culture, which includes politics and economics.

Being King of kings means that Jesus is the President of all presidents, Prime Minister of all prime ministers, not just the King of the Church or the King of kings in the next life. Ephesians 1:17-23 clearly states that His present rule is over all other rulers both in Heaven and on earth.

To summarize, Jesus came to claim His lordship over every kingdom and dominion in Heaven and on earth. He didn't come merely for Israel or the Church, but to establish His Kingdom and to equip His ekklesia to disciple every nation on every continent with His law-word.

The New Covenant Kingdom

There is much confusion today related to the Kingdom of God. Some believe that the Church is the Kingdom of God, but Scripture teaches that the Church functions inside the Kingdom as one of the five major realms of society. (Psalm 24:1 teaches that the whole earth belongs to the Lord, while Colossians 1:13 teaches that Christians are placed into His Kingdom.)

Also, for the sake of clarity, I want to explain the difference between the "Kingdom of God" and the "Kingdom of Heaven." The Kingdom of God is the influence of His sovereign rule over the cosmos or the universe as its creator (see Col. 1:16-17; Ps. 24:1). The Kingdom of Heaven is the location of God's personal dwelling place related to His throne (see Matt. 5:34; Rev. 21:5; 22:1).

I believe that the Kingdom of God, with Jesus enthroned as the King of kings and Lord of lords, is the most important theme in the New Testament. It was the central theme of Jesus' preaching. Mark 1:14-15 says, *"...Jesus came into Galilee, preaching the gospel of the kingdom of God, and saying, The time is fulfilled, and the kingdom of God is at hand: repent ye, and believe the gospel."*

Matthew 13 is devoted entirely to teaching His disciples about the Kingdom. About the parable of the sower, Jesus told the disciples that they couldn't understand its message unless He gave them the ability to *"know the mysteries of the kingdom of Heaven"* (Matt. 13:11). In His explanation of the parable to His disciples, Jesus explained that the problem people have with the Gospel is that they don't understand *"the word of the kingdom"* (Matt. 13:18-19).

Jesus taught many parables to begin to enlighten His disciples concerning the scope of His Kingdom. We can use these parables to broaden our understanding of the Kingdom of God as well.

Parables of the Kingdom

Jesus often used parables that related spiritual and natural laws to human life and the created order to illustrate His Kingdom. This was not a coincidence, but very intentional. By integrating both spiritual and natural laws into these easy-to-understand illustrations, He was demonstrating that His Kingdom consists of the whole created order and not just spiritual or religious issues.

He made use of illustrations from various disciplines of life so that the Kingdom might be understood by people from various backgrounds. The parables are a great place to gain the understanding we need about God's definition of Kingdom.

In parables such as "The Sower and the Seed" in Mark 4:1-20 and "The Wheat and Tares" in Matthew 13:24-30, Jesus used real-life principles regarding the agrarian realm that coincide with spiritual realities. He easily drew illustrations from these pedestrian functions to demonstrate life-changing truths regarding salvation and His Kingdom.

In Matthew 13:33, Jesus told another parable utilizing the culinary art of making bread to teach that His Kingdom is like leaven because it starts off small or hidden but eventually works its influence into every realm of state and society.

"The Parable of the Hidden Treasure," found in Matthew 13:44, says that the Kingdom of Heaven is like treasure hidden in a field, which a man finds and then sells all that he has in order to buy it. "The Parable of the Pearl of Great Price" in Matthew 13:45-46 is similar to the hidden treasure story. It says that the Kingdom of Heaven is like a merchant seeking beautiful pearls. When he finds the most beautiful pearl, he sells all that he has to buy it.

Businesspeople can easily relate to either of these parables because they deal with a person who made a business decision and sold his assets, exchanging them for more valuable property. Being willing to give up everything in exchange for the enormous benefits of serving the Lord is an important part of the Kingdom of God.

A businessperson can also easily relate to "The Parable of the Dragnet," found in Matthew 13:47-50, because quality control regarding product is the main component of having a successful company. When Jesus related how He will choose who enters His eternal Kingdom to the fishing industry, He was making a contemporary business practice relevant to an eternal reality.

If Jesus were preaching on the earth today, He might use the subprime banking mortgage scandal as a way of illustrating how a person who wants to be a disciple of Jesus must count the cost properly before he (or she) decides he (or she) wants to follow Him. He might also use the metaphor of a wolf in sheep's clothing to expose the predatory lending practices of banks who take advantage of people who want to purchase a home.

The Kingdom of God was also the main theme of the apostle Paul's preaching. Paul spent two years preaching *"the kingdom of God"* and *"those things which concern the Lord Jesus Christ"* (Acts 28:31). He emphasized that the central message of Christianity was the Kingdom, echoing the Lord Jesus' lessons about how to access the Father and accomplish our purpose in His Kingdom.

Since the Kingdom encompasses all of creation, it involves every aspect of a person's life and should define his or her worldview. Every kingdom has individuals, families, educational philosophies, political concepts, economic systems, philosophical systems, sociological structures, psychological constructs, judicial systems, and laws that reflect its core values and ethos. Hence, the Kingdom of God involves every aspect of the life of the individual in matters of private faith and public policy. According to Matthew 7:21-27, the main stumbling block in forming a relationship with God is an unwillingness to allow Christ to be Lord in every one of these aspects of one's life.

Misinterpretation of the Kingdom

Several arguments, in response to the position I take in this chapter, are used to justify Christianity's position of nonengagement in transforming culture. In John 18:36, Jesus told Pilate:

My kingdom is not of this world. If My kingdom were of this world, then My servants would fight, so that I should not be delivered to the Jews; but now My kingdom is not from here (NKJV).

To understand this verse we have to examine the context of this conversation between Pilate and Jesus.

Jesus was telling Pilate that His Kingdom did not emanate from this present world system of power and government. Thus He didn't have to resort to fighting with Roman soldiers to fulfill God's Kingdom plan. Jesus was referring to the source and nature of His power; He was not making a statement about disengagement from politics.

People who have misinterpreted this verse fail to see that the following verse abrogates any possible view that Jesus was telling the Church to opt out of politics and social engagement. Jesus told Pilate that His purpose for being born was to be King, a highly unlikely title to call Himself if He was opposed to His followers being engaged in cultural and political issues.

Of course, there are instances when the Church must build a subculture and opt out of the cultural mainstream. For example, when there has been religious persecution, the Church has had to meet in secret locations. The early Church often met in the catacombs during the Roman persecutions; and the Church in modern communist countries has had to meet in people's homes or even in the forest.

Here's another example of when it might be necessary to build a subculture and opt out of the cultural mainstream. If and when our nation ever requires all public schools to adopt a curriculum that pushes alternate forms of family structure and teaches about sexual orientation, I would encourage all pastors to start Christian schools so the children of their members can be educated without unnecessary exposure to aberrant sexual indoctrination.

Many who read Ephesians 2:1-2 and First John 5:19 conclude that God has given satan the right to rule over all the world systems. Thus they believe it's a waste of our time to reform them. I address this issue in my book *Ruling in the Gates:*

> These verses teach that the world system is presently influenced and controlled by the enemy, but nowhere in Scripture does it say that Satan has the right to continue to do this. I contend that Jesus told us in the Lord's Prayer to make earth reflect Heaven—to seek first His kingdom and His righteousness. I believe this means our mission is not simply to disciple people into Heaven, but also to put down the present satanic system and declare, "The kingdom of God is at hand" (Matt. 4:17; 12:28). This means more than casting devils out of people; it means casting devils out of systems, families, neighborhoods, communities, cities and nations. According to Colossians 2:15 Jesus already disarmed Satan; now it's up to the church to displace him![1]

Matthew 4:8-10 is perhaps the most commonly used verse to justify the Church's separation from politics and other aspects of culture that deal with systemic sin. It seems to imply that Jesus agreed with satan when he told Jesus that the kingdoms of the world belonged to him.

Some may interpret this to mean that God gave satan the legal right to do what he wants in regard to politics, economics, and culture. I disagree. Satan obviously has influence over political and societal systems, but Jesus never said that was right. He told satan that every kingdom of this world should submit to the lordship of Christ and worship Him. (And in Luke 4:5-8 Jesus told satan that worship belongs to God alone.) Jesus is the King of kings and Lord of lords, and we are to be His representatives to every nation and to influence every walk of life for His Kingdom.

Applying Kingdom Principles

Our church has been actively working to apply Kingdom principles by serving our city in various realms of life. In the late 1990s I began training about 30 people to practically apply the biblical worldview to economics and politics in our surrounding community. As part of this training I had some of the members work with a local political organization so that they would receive firsthand experience in how politics operate. Other members of this group were placed in important positions with a powerful local leader in state politics. One actually served as the campaign manager for this political leader. Another became the director of a nonprofit organization with a lot of community influence.

Since that time we have also been involved in helping to organize community rallies and events and have had the opportunity to mediate between community leaders and the police department regarding social relations. Furthermore, a number of people from our church, including me, sit in influential positions on local community decision-making boards that affect approximately 200,000 people in two communities. Once a year I am asked to participate in a citywide forum with key religious leaders for the purpose of community understanding.

This past year I was asked to facilitate a meeting with some of the top Jewish, Muslim, Hindu, and other religious leaders for the purpose of finding common ground so that we could better serve our city. I chose the Great Commandment found in Matthew 22:37-40 as the key reference for this prominent religious conference. I was able to then directly influence these key religious leaders with God's Kingdom principles.

This is just a brief snapshot of the ways our church attempts to reflect God's Kingdom rule by not only interceding for our city and its leaders, but by also influencing every realm of life through active involvement and participation.

THINK ON THIS

As we close this section I want to emphasize how important it is to understand the role of our King, to know how to define the word *kingdom,* and to learn how the Church is called to be the key representatives of His Kingdom. As believers, we also need to know the difference between the Kingdom of God and the Kingdom of Heaven.

Please stop and take the time to make sure you have these important principles firmly imbedded in your spirit.

What is the role of our King?

Define the word *kingdom.*

What is the difference between the Kingdom of God and the Kingdom of Heaven?

My hope is that all believers will eventually understand that the main theme in the teachings of both Jesus and Paul was the Kingdom of God, which goes far beyond the good news of salvation. These teachings have vast implications that connect our stewardship of God's Kingdom principles to reaching the whole of the created order.

Christians have much to offer the world concerning the understanding and implementation of God's Kingdom principles in every corner of the earth. Remember, we are called to be salt and light; therefore, we are to be major transformers of every aspect of society.

How can you become salt and light and begin transforming aspects of your own local community?

Begin to think outside the box as to how you can introduce God's Kingdom principles into every area of your daily life.

Endnote

1. Joseph Mattera, *Ruling in the Gates* (Lake Mary, FL: Creation House, 2003), 12.

CHAPTER 6
THE UNIVERSAL TRUTH
OF THE KINGDOM

Jesus said..."I am the way, and the truth, and the life; no one comes to the Father but through Me" (John 14:6 NASB).

Christianity does not merely teach the truth—its understanding forms the actual rational basis for understanding all truth. As we will see in this chapter, the greatest proof of the divine inspiration of the Bible is the impossibility of making rational sense of the world without assuming its worldview. Hence, if we are going to be successful in claiming every sphere of our world for Christ, we must train a new crop of leaders to defend our faith and to "[cast] *down imaginations, and every high thing that exalteth itself against the knowledge of God..."* (2 Cor. 10:5). According to this verse, we have to go beyond merely reforming politics and economics, and we have to get to the very core of our actions and attitudes. We have to deal with our thoughts or presuppositions that underlie our practices in both the private and public arena.

The Bible tells us, *"The fear of the Lord is the beginning of wisdom..."* (Prov. 9:10). We need to use Scripture as our starting point in regards to how we frame our view of life in every realm, including matters pertinent to public policy such as economics, education, family, science, and politics.

Christianity is more than just the practical way to live; it has *the best* moral code and principles for living a productive and meaningful life. In actuality, Christian theism is the precondition for all intelligence because without it all logic, morality, debate, and public policy fall into absurdity.

Francis Schaeffer said, "When I say Christianity is true I mean it is true to total reality—the total of what is, beginning with the central reality, the objective existence of the personal, infinite God."[1] With this profound statement, Schaeffer is saying that Christianity does not just deal with truth related to salvation, but also in matters of the whole created order. Thus mathematics, world history, science, politics, and all other fields have their starting point and purpose inextricably connected to our personal, infinite God.

In John 14:6, when Jesus said that He was the truth and the only way to the Father, He was saying that, apart from knowing Him, practitioners of all the various disciplines of life are operating by function without understanding the purpose. John 1:9 says that Jesus is the *"true Light which gives light to every man coming into the world"* (NKJV). It is only through a personal relationship with Him that we can understand and then effectively implement God's Kingdom principles in every area of life.

Atheists, Agnostics, and Evolutionists

James 1 begins by assuring us that God will give us the wisdom we need to deal with those who wish to debate or negate His Kingdom principles and authority. It says, *"But if any of you lacks wisdom, let him ask of God, who gives to **all** generously and without reproach, and it will be given to him"* (James 1:5 NASB). The stipulation for receiving this wisdom is explained in verses 6-8.

*But he must ask in faith without any doubting, for the one who
doubts is like the surf of the sea, driven and tossed by the wind.
For that man ought not to expect that he will receive anything
from the Lord, being a double-minded man, unstable in all his
ways* (James 1:6-8 NASB).

To ensure that we do not fall into the realm of the unstable and
double-minded, we must study to show ourselves approved and be
familiar with both Scripture and the beliefs of those who seek to
deny the truth (see 2 Tim. 2:15).

The fact that we intuitively understand the concepts of right
and wrong and good and evil and that we expect the sun to shine
every morning, the birds to sing, and a car engine to turn on with
a key confirms that we live in an orderly world perfectly designed
by our Creator. As simple as this may sound, when those who don't
believe in God, such as atheists or agnostics, take these things for
granted, they are actually borrowing from the worldview of a the-
ist or one who believes in God. An antisupernatural, naturalistic
view of the world can't account for the fact that we can predict the
future based on our past observance of set natural laws that demonstrate design rather than chance. (I have even recently heard of
one prominent atheist who calls himself a "cultural Christian" because he said that he functions in life with a sense of innate morality toward fellow humans.)

For example, when one human shows another human more respect than they would a dog or a cat, whether they know it or not,
they are borrowing from a biblical worldview that teaches that humans are the only creatures made in the image and likeness of God
(see Gen. 1:26-27; 9:5-6). When an atheist goes to a funeral and
mourns the loss of a friend or relative, or treats fellow human beings with more dignity and respect than all other creatures, he is
demonstrating an innate belief that humankind has a unique quality that transcends all other creatures. Such a belief cannot be justified by the evolutionary or antisupernaturalistic philosophy,

which teaches that all creatures are essentially equal because humans, like animals, have no spirit or life after physical death.

Furthermore, an atheist has no philosophical grounds for being upset over a politician taking bribes or a robber murdering innocent people. The naturalistic worldview of good and evil is based totally on human opinion and social and cultural constructs. If we all evolved from some primordial soup, then all living things are related, and it would be just as evil to step on a roach as it would be to kill an innocent human being.

The fact that humans have an innate sense of right and wrong is one way to prove that there is a truth that transcends the natural world and gives all human beings a sense of dignity and purpose that a horse or a plant can never experience.

Regarding natural philosophy and its counterpart, evolution, C.S. Lewis says, "Materialism gives us a theory which explained everything else in the whole universe but which made it impossible to believe that our thinking was valid."[2]

That is to say, we either have as our starting point:

(a) a materialistic, impersonal, and random convergence of matter and motion that cannot give an account of science,[3] logic, reason, categories, or grammar;

Or

(b) Christian theism, which alone provides the precondition for all intelligence, not just spiritual things or morality.

Note: I cite Christian theism alone because other theistic religions like Judaism, Islam, and Mormonism have theological and historical inconsistencies that don't comport with fullness of divine revelation found in both the Old and New Testaments.

The Laws of Logic

Either the process of human reason (the law of logic) has only a physical explanation based solely on chemical interactions causing electrical charges that give orders to other nerves in various parts of the body, or it has no physical origination but emanates from our soul giving instructions to our physical brain which then directs various parts of our physical body to act. We can't have it both ways. It seems obvious that human logic is based on immaterial concepts that transcend physical, chemical responses in the brain. For example, if I am imagining an elephant in my mind, it is an immaterial image. If it was physical, the elephant would literally be materially present in my human head.

Science

Truly some of the greatest scientists in history were believers in God. Isaac Newton, for example, wrote more books on theology than he authored on science. The impetus for science came about because men were attempting to discover more about God by studying His creation (see Ps. 111:2).

In the past, the study of science was called "moral philosophy" because it presupposed that there are natural, orderly laws that can be studied and used to not only understand various aspects of our world, but to predict the future path of certain occurrences. The inherent belief that the universe was created and designed by a personal God was the initial basis for the concept of scientific study.

Either the universe was designed with natural laws or it evolved by chance—we can't have it both ways. Scientific experimentation easily fits within the framework of the Christian theistic worldview, but the concept of predicting the future based on the past doesn't rationally equate with a worldview in which the universe was created by the random-chance interrelationship of "matter in motion."

Categories

Categories are a phenomenon that can easily be explained by a worldview in which Jesus holds all things in creation together.[4] We need categories so that we can view the world in a cohesive manner and process all the information that comes to us in an orderly, manageable way.

For example, if I take a reductionist approach, which involves breaking every material thing down to its basic materialistic particulars, it is very difficult to tell the difference between a canary and a parrot because, biologically speaking, they are very similar. They each can fly; they have eyes, a nose, feathers, a beak, and so forth.

To understand how complicated this is philosophically, suppose you have two individual birds that are both classified as canaries, but when you compare them in detail they are very different in regards to their nuance in size, color, and behavior. Yet bird-watchers can immediately tell that both are canaries because of the existence of "canary" categories.

I have fun with this when I ask people to define what a human being is from a biological standpoint. Most will respond that humans have two legs, two eyes, one nose, two ears, and hair and that they cohabit together in communities (something that many other mammals do as well). "So," I ask them, "what is the difference between a human and other mammals?"

Outside of the Christian worldview it would be difficult to describe the difference between a human and an ape. Christians know that humans not only have a particular anatomy but were created in the image and likeness of God, with a soul for self-awareness and a spirit that will exist for eternity.

Names

Along with this concept of categories we also have the concept of "names." Imagine I ask you what your name is, and you tell me "Joe." I could argue and say that if your name is just the syllables that just came out of your mouth, then you are nameless because after it is spoken out of your mouth it is gone forever.

But, because your name is an immaterial category that transcends the physical syllables, once you say your name, all those around you will always know you as "Joe." Your name is now a category that identifies you in some particular way. Names and categories cannot be explained in an atheistic, anti-spiritual worldview because they transcend their material syllabic expression (sounds that are gone once they are spoken).

C.S. Lewis said:

For in order to think, we must claim for our reasoning a validity which is not credible if our own thought is merely a function of our brain and our brain a byproduct of irrational physical process.[5]

The greatest proof of the inspiration of Scripture is the impossibility of the contrary. That is to say, without the worldview of the Bible, we have no rational explanation for the reality that we empirically experience and observe in everyday life.

Propagating the Kingdom of God

Although there are many fine approaches to apologetics, I believe that the method best suited to those propagating the Kingdom of God is the presuppositional approach, which attempts to prove the superiority of Christianity by contrasting the Christian worldview with all other worldviews and belief systems. As a result of demonstrating the superiority of the Christian worldview, we show the relevancy of our faith and are motivated to apply the Kingdom principles of the Bible to every sphere of life.

The two great giants who developed this method of apologetics were Abraham Kuyper and Cornelius Van Til. Kuyper held that faith is the prerequisite for all learning and that the starting point of all argumentation is the self-attesting authority of Scripture (see Prov. 9:10).

Faith makes scholarship possible because belief about things always precedes examination of the evidence. Even when Christian and non-Christian thinkers agree about particular phenomena in creation, they disagree about principles such as the doctrine of Creation itself. This is because they approach the study of the world with mutually opposing assumptions.

Van Til summarizes his method by saying that Christian theism is the precondition for all intelligence. Van Til would say anti-theism must presuppose theism to prove atheism. In other words, if an atheist were to debate a Christian, the atheist would lose simply by showing up for the debate. He would have to employ the facets of reason, intelligence, logic, and rhetoric to even participate in such a debate, which is something his worldview doesn't allow for.

Greg Bahnsen wrote:

The Christian, as did Tertullian, must contest the very principles of his opponent's position. The only "proof" of the Christian position is that unless its truth is presupposed there is no possibility of "proving" anything at all. The actual state of affairs as preached by Christianity is the necessary foundation of "proof" itself.[6]

Similarly, Philip Johnson said:

People who start from the wrong foundation don't make just one error, they create a tower of errors.[7]

Our logic cannot supply its own beginning. Logic is merely a way of reasoning correctly from premises to conclusions. The premises must come from elsewhere. Rationalism is inherently self-defeating, because the rationalist must pretend to derive his first premises as biological reasoning, which always rests on other premises. Empiricism faces the same dilemma when it becomes a total system because the empiricist always needs to know more than he can observe.[8]

A Clash of Worldviews

When one analyzes the nature of reality and debate, all argumentation is really about a clash of worldviews and presuppositions, not based on piecemeal data. A person's presuppositions (or basic assumptions) will act as a filter and thus determine how they interpret the world and the data that comes into their mind.

A great modern example of this is the famous O.J. Simpson criminal trial of the 1990s. After viewing the same evidence, most African-Americans believed he was innocent while most Caucasian-Americans thought he was guilty. Even though both groups were exposed to the same data regarding Mr. Simpson, they came to opposite conclusions because they filtered the information that came to them differently due to different perspectives regarding the judicial system.

For a worldview to be true, it must comport with reality and the created order. Naturalism, Buddhism, Islam, Mormonism, and all other world religions cannot claim to do this because they are contrary to the revealed will of God found in the Old and New Testaments.

Although Islam, Mormonism, and other theistic religions can use most of the same arguments that Christians use against naturalism, they fall short because of logical, historical, and theological problems. They violate the law of noncontradiction when they add to the Bible's revelation. Their foundational belief systems are either polytheistic or are based on something other than on the revelation of Jesus Christ as Lord. For more information on this, read *Cults, World Religions, and You* by Ken Boa, *The Kingdom of the Cults* by Walter Martin, and *Always Ready* by Dr. Greg Bahnsen.

We can conclude, however, that there is no such thing as neutrality. Either Christ is Lord over everything in the created order or He isn't Lord at all. If we can logically prove something can exist outside of the Lordship of Christ, then the Christian faith isn't true, and we can throw our Bibles away.[9]

A Christian cannot even conclude that mathematics is neutral. Addition, subtraction, division, and multiplication were all introduced by God in Genesis 1. Mathematics, like everything else in the created order, makes no sense without a transcendent purpose attached to it from its designer. It is meant to glorify God by supplying human beings with the concepts to facilitate our reasoning within the laws of sowing and reaping so that we can properly steward our lives and this planet to the glory of God.

The Hindu concept of reality is an example of how other major worldviews and philosophies are left without a rational explanation of mathematics. They teach a form of pantheism and radical monism that says "all is one and god is all" and in which any differences are *maya* or illusions.

James Nickel, in his book *Mathematics: Is God Silent?*, writes about this:

The problem with this position [of radical monism] is that if everything is one, then there can be no science and mathematics. For mathematics to work you must have a philosophy of plurality, i.e., that there are many things. As long as one attempts to explain everything in terms of one principle, then any remaining diversity will be a problem. An ancient example of radical pluralism is the Greek philosopher Democritus. He embraced an atomistic theory of matter in which all things are composed of minute, invisible, indestructible particles of pure matter, which move about eternally in infinite empty space. A modern example is the nominalism or empiricism of Western civilization where only individual objects or particulars have real existence. You can experience five dollars or five soft drinks, but you cannot abstract from these experiences the universal concept of fiveness. In order to do mathematics you must resolve the thorny metaphysical question of the "one and the many." This tension is resolved and answered in the nature of the ontological trinity, the eternal one and the many.[10]

Winning a Non-Christian

In order to bring a non-Christian to a place of understanding a biblical worldview, you should learn to effectively use the following steps:

1. Identify the other person's underlying worldview or basic assumptions regarding reality.

2. Point out the internal inconsistencies of their worldview.

3. Get them to admit that their worldview is illogical.

4. Illustrate how Christian theism has the only logical worldview that comports with reality.

faulty premises and accept

how such a conversation be-an might go using the steps

g with his neighbor Sheila, considers herself a spiritual

consider yourself a spiritual

s. "Everything points to the . We are all really one with the universe, you know. All the problems we face in this world are really because of the illusions of differences we perceive between people and nature. If we could all just come to this understanding, the world would be a much better place."

John then asks his first probing question, "So then how do you explain right and wrong or good and evil?"

Sheila passionately responds, "The existence of good and evil is really an illusion perpetrated on us by narrow-minded religious fanatics who train their children a certain way which they label as right or good. Everything that doesn't agree with them is wrong or evil, so they try to influence society according to their personal religious beliefs."

John, perceiving from this that Sheila is really a believer in New Age Pantheism (which says that the whole universe is one and that all is god and god is all), asks, "Do you believe then that 2+2 will ever equal 5?"

Sheila quickly responds with, "No, of course not; 2+2 always equals 4. What does that have to do with anything?"

John begins to explain saying, "In mathematics you have to believe in the fact that there is one right answer to the equation. If we were to follow the line of thinking that you were just describing, then 2+2 could sometimes equal 5 or 6 or 7 depending on what we were adding up and why. Think of the confusion this would cause in purchasing daily items if there was no consistency in the pricing. For me, $2.00 + $2.00 equals $4.00, but for the next person in the checkout line $2.00 + $2.00 only equals $3.00 because of some difference in our circumstances."

Sheila appears a little confused and says, "Well, that just doesn't make any sense. Everyone knows that 2+2 equals 4."

John shakes his head in agreement and then continues by asking her, "Alright then, do you think it would be good for me to punch you in the face?"

Sheila quickly responds, "Of course not."

John asks, "Why isn't it a good thing to do?"

Sheila answers, "Because it would hurt me physically."

John says, "But what if hitting you in the face makes me feel good by enabling me to express my pent-up frustrations and anger? Doesn't that make it alright since it is good for me?"

Sheila seems to be struggling to respond. "Well...I just know I don't want you to hit me in the face."

John decides to take this example even further, asking, "What if I not only hit you in the face, but I go about habitually attempting to hurt other people physically and maybe even killing someone? Would I be a good person or a bad person if I explained that doing so made me feel good?"

Sheila admits, "Well, in this case maybe what is good for you would be bad for me."

John, seeing his opportunity to press his point, asks, "Is it wrong to invade another's personal property and take what they have worked hard to achieve so that I can feel better about myself? How can one person be bad for doing that while another is not?"

Sheila now shakes her head and says, "Well, maybe we do need a few laws or rules so that innocent people don't get hurt just because someone else is hurting."

John feels he can go back to the subject of religion now that she has seen there is some inconsistency in her spiritual belief system, "In the same way that 2+2 will never equal 5, Islam and Christianity cannot both be true at the same time. Islam teaches that Jesus was a created being, and Christianity teaches that Jesus is uncreated because He is God the Son. New Agers believe that Jesus was the Christ for the past 2,000 years, but Christianity teaches that Jesus is the only eternal Christ or Anointed One that is the Savior of the world."

John sees that Sheila is beginning to get the picture so he says, "If we believe that all religions are one, then we must also believe that God is illogical and irrational or just can't make up His mind. If the God we serve is that irrational or confused, then we may as well say that the human language is useless, work is useless, love is useless, relationships and family are useless, and even our thinking is useless because these are all based on logical, orderly, and rational behavior."

Sheila admits that she sees that all religions must not be one. "But how can you know for sure which one is the right one, the one that has the real truth?"

John then shares his testimony regarding his conversion to Christ and why he now believes Jesus is the only Savior of the world. He concludes by telling Sheila, "Since I asked Jesus in my heart as my Lord and Savior, I have received the assurance of eternal life, forgiveness of sins, and a sense of purpose that gives me great joy and fulfillment, even in the midst of trials and suffering."

Sheila admits, "You do seem to handle a crisis a lot differently than most people I know. I've wanted to ask you about that."

John smiles and says, "Sheila, you can have this same assurance and peace in your life. Jesus will forgive you if you admit you are a sinner who has broken God's moral standards of right and wrong. Do you want to experience this forgiveness?"

Sheila responds in the affirmative, and John prays with her as she asks Jesus into her life, beginning a new journey in which not only her behavior, but also her basic assumptions about life and reality, will be totally transformed.

As we move forward in the Kingdom of God, we have to see our faith as the *only consistent, comprehensive, and coherent worldview* that has the ability to comport with reality. Once we are secure in who we are and able to effectively explain why we believe what we do, we can begin applying God's Kingdom principles to all areas of our lives, even economics and politics.

By using the tools presented in this chapter, we can present truth in a way that will show the world what the truth is and set them free from the false doctrines and mindsets that have brought such confusion and disorder to our world.

THINK ON THIS

As we conclude this chapter, it is important for us to understand why the Christian faith has the answer for all reality and is not limited to just spiritual things. The biblical worldview should always be the starting point for defending our faith. The greatest proof of the divine inspiration of the Bible is the impossibility of interpreting reality apart from its presuppositions.

We need to understand that even an atheist has to borrow from the Christian worldview in order to attempt to prove his or her atheism. The most effective way to defend Christianity against any of its opponents is by engaging in a worldview comparison to see which view is more consistent with observable reality.

Think of a scenario either from the workplace or your neighborhood where you wanted to explain your faith in God but were met with arguments you could not convincingly reply to. Replay that scenario, but this time use what you have learned in this chapter to bring Christianity's opponent to a saving knowledge of Jesus Christ.

If you find you still have a problem in this area, spend time studying how Jesus handled confrontation with the Pharisees and teachers of the Law. Read through the parables and see how Jesus used familiar everyday examples to help His listeners understand what He was teaching them.

Become familiar with other religions so you can recognize the "key phrases" and know specifically how to counter their false doctrines and mindsets. Just telling them that they are wrong and that they are going to hell will not win them to Christ. Rehearse some scenarios with each religious belief system you study and become proficient in presenting Christianity to unbelievers.

It would be a good idea to begin keeping a journal to record your thoughts and effectiveness in this pursuit of taking God's truth into all of the world.

Endnotes

1. Francis Schaeffer, *A Christian Manifesto* (Wheaton, IL: Crossway Books, 1982), 19-20.

2. Charles Colson and Nancy Pearcey, *How Now Shall We Live?* (Carol Stream, IL: Tyndale House, 2004), 419.

3. Science bases empirical experimentation on predicting the future due to past observation—something a world based on random chance and contingencies cannot do logically.

4. Colossians 1:17 and Hebrews 1:3 teach that in Christ the whole universe holds together.

5. Charles Colson and Nancy Pearcey, *How Now Shall We Live?* (Carol Stream, IL: Tyndale House Publishers, 2004), 422.

6. Greg Bahnsen, *Van Til's Apologetic: Readings and Analysis* (Phillipsburg, NJ: P&R Publishing, 1998), 730.

7. Philip Johnson, *The Right Questions: Truth, Meaning & Public Debate* (Downers Grove, IL: InterVarsity Press, 2004), 66.

8. *Ibid.*, 89.

9. The Bible teaches that Christ created and designed the universe. Rationally we can conclude that everything that exists, including all truth, both in the seen and unseen realms, is interconnected because it all shares the same genesis (i.e., "In the beginning, God...").

10. James Nickel, *Mathematics: Is God Silent?* (Vallecito, CA: Ross House Books, 2001), 230-231.

CHAPTER 7
THE ECONOMICS OF THE KINGDOM

When we first started Resurrection Church in 1984 in the Sunset Park section of Brooklyn, New York, our church consisted mostly of poor young Hispanic families and singles, a large percentage of them on welfare. There was only one person in our whole church who owned their own home. In 1991 my wife and I became only the second family to own a home, but all this changed dramatically when I started preaching on the Kingdom of God and learned that poverty is primarily a mindset that has to be broken.

This erroneous mindset was soon shattered when the congregation heard me declare that God has called them as His ministers to influence every realm of life. We learned that God has called His Church to have dominion, to be the head and not the tail, to lend and not to borrow (see Deut. 28).

Within a few years many people in our church purchased homes, and I am not aware of any committed members losing their homes during the housing meltdown between 2006 and 2008. After three years of preaching the Kingdom, Resurrection Church was able to purchase its own building, completely paying it off in only seven years. Our congregation now sits in a debt-free multi-million-dollar property.

There are numerous examples of families in our church who have been impacted by the Kingdom message. Most of those who were on welfare have climbed up the financial ladder to middle class, many becoming very wealthy with assets well into the millions.

One young man, Angel, was the teenage head of one of the most notorious street gangs in our area, making over one million dollars a year selling drugs. After his conversion I prophesied over him that God was going to make him a multimillionaire within a few years if he would fully surrender to God and give up his drug dealing. Within two years he was creating wealth by purchasing and renovating properties, then leasing them to the state for use as rehab centers. And he was back to making a million a year.

Another young man, David, was only seven years old when we began picking him up for our Children of the City Saturday sessions. He came from a broken family that lived on welfare in a drug-infested apartment complex. Today he is the married father of three and is making a six-figure income working for Goldman Sachs in New York City. He also serves as one of the church ministers, often preaching on Sunday to our growing congregation.

Richard had a blue-collar mentality, satisfied with making between $50,000 and $60,000 a year as a doorman. His wife Yvette worked for a local mortgage business. In the early 2000s, Richard took a step of faith, quit his job as a doorman, and began working in real estate with a partner. Soon he was making as much in one month as he did the whole year as a doorman. Yvette opened her own business, and today she owns her own bank and specializes in helping people save their homes from foreclosure.

Poverty or Prosperity

For the past few decades, the Church as a whole has debated whether or not we should embrace poverty or prosperity. Thankfully, the movement has increasingly affirmed the Church's monetary growth so that it becomes a catalyst to expand Christendom. But this new thinking goes against our traditional mentality of "dying to the flesh." It also rubs up against the rampant fiscal abuse that has marred church history, causing many Christians to reexamine their beliefs surrounding wealth and poverty.

Since the founding of the monastic movements in the Catholic church, many have thought it pious to forsake all worldly possessions, labeling it "dying to the flesh." This belief, popularized by the begging friars and St. Francis of Assisi, led many in the Church to think it was spiritual to take a vow of poverty (something the Roman Catholic church requires of their clergy to this day). Some medieval saints even thought it better to not bathe, to sleep on wooden planks, and to limit their intake and variety of food and drink.

However, as the Church has progressed into liberty, we have come to realize that creating income for the advancement of the Kingdom is God's idea, rather than a sinful deed.

Blessed to Be a Blessing

I truly believe it is God's will to prosper His people so that we can perpetuate the Kingdom on the earth. I finally came to the conclusion that if I only believed God for just enough to get by, I would be perpetuating a spirit of poverty rather than living nobly for the Kingdom. After all, just believing God for the minimum that we need means we won't have the financial ability to bless others.

The Bible teaches that we should work and have enough to be a blessing to others (see Eph. 4:28). The believer will either be a blessing or a burden by creating wealth or by always being in need of it. I would rather be like my Father in Heaven who is the greatest blesser of all. Quoting Jesus in Acts 20:35, Paul said, *"It is more blessed to give than to receive."*

One of the most popular biblical passages in history is the story of the Good Samaritan found in Luke 10:25-37. In this story, Jesus praised the Samaritan man who stopped to aid a victim of a violent mugging. The Samaritan then provided him with medical care and paid for his stay at an inn until he was fully recovered.

This story is one of the greatest proponents for why believers should financially prosper. Only a prosperous person would be able to afford to put someone up in an inn indefinitely while also paying for his medical and food expenses. Those of us who have a "just enough" financial mentality would not qualify to be the Good Samaritan in this story. After restoring someone to health, as the Good Samaritan did, it would be easy to witness to that person of God's great love.

Deuteronomy 8:18 says that it is God *"who gives you the ability to produce wealth, and so confirms His covenant, which He swore to your forefathers, as it is today"* (NIV). Psalm 35:27 says that God takes pleasure in the prosperity of His *servants*. He wants us to learn how to give, get, manage, save, and invest money.[1]

God hates financial oppression, and He desires justice for the poor, widows, orphans, and aliens. He will bless those who prioritize His Kingdom finances and those who manage their money well. This can only be done when Christians go from a rights-centered concept of prosperity to a stewardship-centered concept of servanthood.

I believe that one of the main reasons why the United States has prospered is because we have become a safe haven for millions of immigrants seeking refuge from oppressive societies. We have also been the greatest benefactor in the history of the world, sending out hundreds of billions of dollars in loans and grants every year to developing nations and nonprofit relief organizations.

The truth is that the money and possessions we have are not our own. God is only entrusting us with them so that we can steward His Kingdom on the earth. When we view ourselves as God's treasurers instead of possessors of wealth, we will experience the ability to create wealth.

For example, one of the leading families of our church heard from God that they were to sow all of the money that they had saved for their child's college education toward paying off the church's mortgage. God told them that if they obeyed, He would pay off the rest of their personal mortgage, which was more than double what they sowed into the church. Within the year, the husband closed the largest deal in the history of his company, which enabled him to fully pay off his house. Thus, if in our hearts we possess nothing and are God's stewards (or treasurers) in spite of an abundance of material possessions, then we will have the proper attitude to give what God wants us to give when He wants us to give it. Doing so will release God to give us what He wants us to have when He wants us to have it!

God's Stewards

In Luke 16:1-13, Jesus taught the principles of stewardship that release God's full financial blessing. The key to being godly stewards of the wealth and assets that God has given us is found in the following portion of "The Parable of the Shrewd Manager."

> *He who is faithful in a very little thing is faithful also in much; and he who is unrighteous in a very little thing is unrighteous also in much. Therefore if you have not been faithful in the use of unrighteous wealth, who will entrust the true riches to you? And if you have not been faithful in the use of that which is another's, who will give you that which is your own?* (Luke 16:10-12 NASB).

I believe that pastors and church leaders should encourage a *culture* of wealth in our churches and ministries. We need to empower our members to have a spirit of excellence in their jobs that will lead to promotion. We also need to encourage those with an entrepreneurial spirit to start up their own Kingdom businesses.

I believe the quickest and easiest way to leverage influence in a region is for Christians and Church-led organizations to meet some of the needs of their community, thus releasing favor with God and man through acts of service.

Our local church started a community-based outreach called Children of the City. Through counseling, human resource networking, and educational support, we have successfully served thousands of at-risk children and their families since 1981 and positively impacted our local community. As a result, key political, community, and business leaders have been falling over each other trying to help us continue to make a difference.

For example, one billionaire is willing to purchase a multimillion dollar facility to aid us in the development of a charter school. A prominent Catholic high school president has offered us free use of their 30-million-dollar facility for numerous after-school and night-school programs. Our programs are 95 percent supported by non-Christian private donors, foundations, or city and state aid. Since 2001, this has totaled millions of dollars and far exceeds our local church's budget and financial abilities.

Once we show that we can be faithful with little, God, who owns *"the cattle upon a thousand hills"* (Ps. 50:10), will give us what would take hundreds of years to earn. When it comes to accessing *"the wealth of the sinner"* (Prov. 13:22), God's favor is the greatest key for releasing finances to the righteous.

According to the great North African Church father Tertullian, serving communities was also the main strategy in the Church of the first few centuries. It led to the penetration and saturation of the whole Roman Empire. Taunting the Roman Emperor, Tertullian said:

> We are but of yesterday, but we have filled every place among you—cities, islands, fortresses, towns, market places, the very camp, tribes, companies, palace, senate, forum—we have left nothing to you but the temples of your gods.[2]

Dr. Ray Bakke makes this observation:

> Early Christians penetrated the whole city, but not by merely claiming space for Christian buildings or programs of their own. They penetrated everybody else's instead![3]

Money is only important because it gives us power and influence so that we can purchase what we need to fulfill our vision. When we learn to serve and love others, we immediately tap into the most powerful principle of Kingdom economics, which is using God's resources to transform nations.

Deuteronomy 8:18 states that God gives us power to obtain wealth so that He may establish His covenant in the earth. God issued an admonition to Israel in Deuteronomy 8:11, warning them against arrogantly forgetting Him once all their needs were met in the land of promise. He went on to say that the reason for wealth is not self-gratification, but for the establishment of God's covenant. The covenantal interaction of God and His people grants us a proper view of money:

1. Wealth is given to the believer for the sake of advancing the Kingdom.

2. Money is thus directly connected to the establishment of the Gospel.

3. Money is a stewardship issue for the Church.

We can then conclude that wealth is not given to a person for the sake of comfort, convenience, or self-gratification, but for Kingdom purposes. With this in mind, we realize that we need to go from a rights-centered Gospel to a stewardship-centered Gospel. We need to shift from claiming prosperity for ourselves to believing that God releases wealth to His people *so that* we can manage the planet and establish His Kingdom principles in every realm of society. God promises that our needs will automatically be met above and beyond what we ask or think if we will seek first His Kingdom and His way of doing things (see Eph. 3:20; Matt. 6:25-33).

Business as a Calling

Too often Christians have believed traditional "sacred versus secular" lies that say having money, especially too much money, is sinful. But the Bible states that it is the *"love* of money" that is sin, not the money itself (1 Tim. 6:10).

Michael Novak's book, *Business as a Calling,* is one example of teaching that bridges the gap between stewardship, ethics, and wealth creation. Novak says that in the past 200 years, wealth creation has tended to focus exclusive attention on means and methods rather than on purposes.

> Economics and business faculties...have been complacently concerned almost exclusively with *means* rather than with *ends—* which, often enough, they have been quite content to leave to ministers, bishops, confessors, moralists, and other (as they see things) more woolly headed thinkers.[4]

There has also been an unfortunate dichotomy between business and morals, making business a secular endeavor rather than looking at it as a sacred calling. Novak states:

> Half of the pleasure from the business calling derives from a sense that the system of which it is a part is highly beneficial to the human race, morally sound, and one of the great social achievements of all time. The other half is personal—finding purpose and meaning in what one does.[5]

God never meant wealth creation to be separate from the service and benefit of humanity. Money should have a moral attachment. Wealth should be viewed as a means of empowering fellow human beings to become effective and productive citizens in the Kingdom. When someone makes money just for the sake of having a lot of it, much of the intrinsic joy that God designed us to walk in is taken away.

Economic Systems

Now that we have a proper biblical view of wealth, we must ask how we can go about solving issues that surround poverty and wealth in our society. For the most part, there is a divide between those who believe in a socialist, large central government method of ministering to the poor and those who believe in the free market principles of capitalism in which aid comes not from political entities but from families, churches, and private organizations. With either position, biblical quandaries arise.

Socialism

In a socialist structure, a minority of people seize political power over the populace with the central government providing for all the necessities of the individual. This violates Second Thessalonians 3:10, which states that a person who does not work should not eat, thereby equating economic worth with individual effort. That is to say, an able-bodied adult should not receive financial benefits if he or she is not earning it with work. I have found that when you give somebody something they don't earn, they usually don't appreciate it.

The welfare system in this country has produced an entitlement mentality in which millions of people expect to receive money from the State even if they are not working. Not only is that not biblically sound, but it actually hurts people in the long run because receiving something for nothing hurts their self-esteem. Since they aren't contributing anything, they have no sense of ownership in their community or city.

Those who espouse socialism often cite Acts 2:44-45 as the reasoning behind their belief system because believers sold all their possessions and then redistributed the wealth to every believer equally. The problem with making this the norm is that it doesn't fit with the rest of the Bible. Owning private property is expected in Isaiah 65:22, Jeremiah 32:42-44, Micah 4:4, Luke 13:13-15, and in the tenth commandment in Exodus 20:17.

The 3,000 people who were saved and added to the Church in Acts 2 were visitors from other countries. Consequently they didn't have a permanent place to live or enough money or food to last more than a few days (see Acts 2:9-11). Thus, the believers living in Jerusalem needed to share their possessions with their new-found brothers and sisters so that they could stay and be established in the faith.

We must also remember that socialism embraces humanism, which does not believe in the fallen nature of humankind. An egalitarian economic structure can only work in a world without envy, jealousy, or lust for power.

One of the ways that Marxists would take over a country was to create class warfare causing division between the bourgeoisie (owners of property) and the proletariat (the working class). The working class was incited to revolt against the upper wealthy class so that their property and wealth could be redistributed evenly among the masses.

Unfortunately, when you take away the monetary incentive for work by giving every person an equal amount, production goes down drastically and the economies of these nations eventually collapse.[6]

Capitalism

On the other hand, the problem with raw capitalism is that the bottom line of this approach is to make more and more money. Money becomes the end instead of a means to an end.

In Kingdom economics, one creates wealth within a free market, yet the goal is not merely the accumulation of money, but to finance the Kingdom and empower believers so that the earth will be filled with the knowledge of God. Matthew 25:14-46 teaches that God rewards those who properly steward their talents and that Jesus will judge us based on how we steward our resources to minister to the poor and the powerless.

As I am writing this chapter, the economic systems of the United States are virtually collapsing because human greed utilized predator lending practices. Unscrupulous banks, motivated solely by economic gain, granted mortgages to millions of low-income people even though they couldn't afford it long term. This clearly exemplifies the biblical law of reaping from exactly what is sown.

The law of sowing and reaping, found in Second Corinthians 9:6-15, teaches that individuals should be motivated by the rewards of reaping according to what they have sown. This distinguishes the creative entrepreneur or hardworking person from the unmotivated or lazy person. God does not favor a person simply because he or she is poor, but rewards those who understand how to multiply their wealth through proper stewardship (see Lev. 19:15).

The Bible actually teaches that God decides who He gives finances to based on their ability to manage and create wealth. The Lord will not pour a lot of money into folks who have no clue how to handle their finances (see Matt. 25:13-30). Jesus actually says in Matthew 25:29 that He will take away from those who have been financially foolish and give to those who have been financially prudent.

Thus, the two basic criteria for receiving God's blessing of wealth are putting God's Kingdom first in all that you do and knowing how to properly manage wealth so that you can be a blessing to others and advance His Kingdom on the earth.

Wealth Management

When Joyce and I got married, we lived on a "no frills" budget. We never went on vacations, only had used furniture and didn't buy new clothes. We saved as much as possible while still giving our tithes and offerings to our local church. Consequently, we were able to purchase a house during the early 1990s when very few people in our church and community were able to afford one. Because we have handled our money well, we presently have more in assets and savings than many others who make far more than we do. Most people make the mistake of adjusting their budgets so they can spend more as they earn more. Only those who invest their money where it will appreciate will have wealth when they retire and leave an inheritance to their children's children, as we are instructed to do in Proverbs 13:22.

If Christians are going to be in the place where God can trust us with most of the world's resources, we have to do more than claim that the wealth of the wicked will be given to the righteous. We need to have a multigenerational wealth-creation plan that involves not only leaving an inheritance for our children's children, but also teaching them how to give, get, keep, and save for the future. In other words, believers have to master the principles of giving through tithes, offerings, alms, and firstfruits, and then teach these important principles to their children.

This includes putting into practice the principles of saving, investing, money management, and wealth creation. We must learn how to invest in things that appreciate rather than depreciate in value. For example, instead of spending an inordinate amount of money on a brand-new car that immediately depreciates in value, buy a less expensive later-model vehicle and then invest the difference in real estate, which has a history of appreciating in value.

The Tithe

Starting with the Book of Genesis, the giving of 10 percent of one's income to God has been a foundational principle related to the worship of God (see Gen. 4:4; 14:20; 28:22). It has also been the primary source of funding for His Kingdom work on the earth.

There is presently a teaching that is gaining traction among Christians that asserts that the giving of tithes is no longer a requirement in the New Testament Church. Two of the most common reasons for this belief are:

1. Tithing is under the law; thus it is no longer required in the New Covenant.

2. Tithing is not specifically taught in the New Testament.

The giving of tithes is not one of the cardinal beliefs necessary for redemption, but it is still an important issue that we must grapple with as we study Kingdom economics. Although these two arguments seem persuasive on the surface, I believe Scripture proves tithing is still a requirement in this present Kingdom age.

It Predates the Law

The principle of giving God the first portion of our income or blessings was instituted centuries before the law of Moses. Thus the giving of tithes is not "under the law" because it predates the law. It was handed down from Adam and Eve to their children; it was practiced by Abraham; and it was part of a vow that Jacob made to God (see Gen. 4:4; 14:20; 28:20-22). All of this occurred before God gave the law to Moses.

It Was Assumed

The New Testament did not have to teach tithing because the early Church was Jewish. The Old Testament was their text, and thus tithing was already assumed. The Book of Acts teaches us that the early Church was made up of devout Jewish believers, which further shows that tithing was already an assumed practice (see Acts 2:5; 21:20).

If tithing is no longer in force because it was not specifically taught in the New Testament, then, by following this line of reasoning, we can also say that homosexuality, bestiality, and incest are acceptable since Jesus never specifically taught against these sins (see Lev. 18:22-23).

It Was Taught and Implied

Tithing was either taught or implied in the New Testament. Jesus actually taught His followers to tithe (see Matt. 23:23). In Romans 2:22, Paul condemned the robbing of temples, which Malachi 3:8-11 seems to indicate had to do with holding back the tithe. The

Jews were generally never guilty of literally robbing the temple, so this verse in Romans must point to the withholding of the food from the storehouse. First Corinthians 16:2 also implies that giving is based on a percentage of a person's income.

It Was Carried Over

Old Testament principles for giving have been carried over to the New Testament. Thus we can apply the Old Testament laws regarding what to do with the tithe to modern circumstances.

The Spirit is now poured out on all flesh, and all believers can enter the Holy of Holies by the blood of Christ. Therefore, one central location (the temple) is no longer applicable for worship (see Heb. 10:19-23). When there was no central tabernacle or single location for worship, the tithe was to be left with the elders at the gates. When the distance to the temple was too far to travel to give the tithe, it was to be left in decentralized locations across the nation with the elders at the gates (see Deut. 14:24-29).

These principles regarding what to do with the tithe fit the pattern of the New Testament since local churches were spread across the globe. In First Corinthians 16:2 Paul instructs believers in local churches to give proportionately to what they made—which, in biblical context, implies the tithe. In Malachi 3:8-14, the Lord commanded the tithe to be brought to the storehouse. In principle the storehouse seems to fit local churches best because of their need to store money in order to fulfill their divine mandate to take care of God's people and preach the Gospel.

Kingdom Taxation

Taxation is not a word we generally associate with Kingdom policy; however, we see from reading the Scriptures that, in principle, the tithe was equivalent to what we would call taxes today. It was used to support projects and categories of people sanctioned by the nation of Israel. For example, in Numbers 3:47 we find a poll (head) tax that God instructed Moses to collect (most likely) for the maintenance of the sanctuary. Deuteronomy 14:29 taught that the tithe would go to support the Levites (state-sponsored ministers), strangers, the fatherless, and widows. In the United States, Social Security, Medicare, and emergency state aid all come from citizen taxation.

Proverbs 3:9 says to honor the Lord with your firstfruits. There are various other offerings in addition to the tithe that are mentioned throughout the Old Testament.

This money was to be used:

1. To support the Levites who served in the tabernacle as shown in Numbers 18:24, First Corinthians 9:14, and First Timothy 5:17.

2. To support aliens, the fatherless, and widows as shown in Deuteronomy 14:29, James 1:27, First Timothy 5:3-4, and Acts 2:45.

3. To build or maintain the sanctuary as shown in Exodus 25:1-8 and Numbers 3:47. (Note: The early Church was not involved in building church buildings because they met in the synagogues and in their homes.)

Although this tax policy was designed for theocratic Israel, I believe these Kingdom economic principles should be used in the future when Christians are in a position to truly disciple a nation.

If we were to apply these Kingdom principles to our modern day, there would be a flat tax policy of approximately 10 percent for all, irrespective of position or income level. The flat tax policy would practically do away with the need for the IRS and all their convoluted tax laws and bureaucracy. I say this because of the fact that in Israel everyone proportionately paid the same amount in tithes irrespective of their personal income. The current American progressive tax structure mandates people to pay more as their income increases. If we were to incorporate a "flat tax" in this country, its simplistic system would do away with the need for so many tax attorneys, accountants, and bureaucracies related to the Internal Revenue Service.

In addition, it would greatly aid the economy because the tax burden would be substantially reduced. Sales tax, capital gains tax, inheritance tax, and marriage tax penalties would be cut out. The poor would not be given exceptions, and tax loopholes for the rich would not be allowed. Yet, in the long run, big corporations would save hundreds of billions of dollars every year since hiring expensive tax accountants and lawyers would no longer be necessary.

The Poor

Since the 1960s, we have seen public assistance programs or welfare spiral out of control, and many have found ways to take advantage of this faulty system. Some work undetected or "off the books" while still collecting welfare checks. Others just refuse to work at all, fearing a loss of their free state support. Couples choose living together over marriage because two reported incomes would mean no more welfare checks.

Millions of people are kept within the cycle of poverty by the current welfare system. When we continually give people free handouts without proper checks and balances, we actually hurt their self-esteem and put a cap on their economic potential. If the Prodigal Son had lived in today's economic culture, when he ran out of money, instead of repenting, he would have merely enrolled in a state-subsidized entitlement program that would have empowered his profligate lifestyle.

In Leviticus 19:9-10, the rich were told to leave the edges of their fields unharvested so that the poor could glean food for themselves. Proverbs continually warned that the lazy would go hungry (see Prov. 13:4,18; 19:15; 20:13; 28:19). Those with economic means were commanded in Exodus 22:25 and Leviticus 25:35-37 to give no-interest loans to the poor. However, in Matthew 25:27, interest loans in general were expected in business deals. Loans had to expire every seven years, however, as prescribed in Deuteronomy 15:1-2 and 9-10.

The economic principles for the poor in the Kingdom of God were balanced. While the tithe and interest-free loans were used to aid the poor, the recipients were still expected to make an honest living by "gleaning" for their produce.

In our contemporary culture, we can see similarities to these biblical principles with the shift from welfare to workfare programs, in which all able-bodied recipients of public assistance must work a full-time job to continue to receive state funding. Initiated first by Mayor Rudy Giuliani in the 1990s, this new policy has done wonders by drastically reducing the welfare rolls in New York City without unemployment increasing. Many former welfare recipients acquired legitimate jobs after they knew that they had to work anyway.

If we are going to have a view of finances that is consistent with Scripture, our approach should always empower others rather than just looking out for ourselves or merely giving other people handouts.

A good man leaves an inheritance for his children's children, but a sinner's wealth is stored up for the righteous (Proverbs 13:22).

THINK ON THIS

Read Deuteronomy 8:18.

What is God's view of wealth creation? What is the difference between a rights-centered Gospel and a stewardship-centered Gospel?

What is the purpose of the tithe?

What is God's method of helping the poor?

What are your thoughts regarding how and why God would want to bless you financially?

Endnotes

1. The story of Joseph in Genesis 37-50 illustrates how saving money can position a person to be a blessing to God's people in a time of economic scarcity.

2. Mark Galli, "Tertullian: Pugnacious Defender of Faith," *Today's Christian Magazine*, 39.1 (January/February 2001), 15, http://www.christianitytoday.com/tc/2001/001/12.15.html (accessed December 14, 2007).

3. Ray Bakke, *A Theology as Big as the City* (Downers Grove, IL: InterVarsity Press, 1997), 193.

4. Michael Novak, *Business as a Calling: Work and the Examined Life* (New York: Free Press, 1996), 4-5.

5. *Ibid.*, 15.

6. For a textbook example of this, study what happened in the former Soviet Union.

CHAPTER 8
THE PRAYERS OF THE KINGDOM

Pray, then, in this way: "Our Father who is in heaven, hallowed by Your name. Your Kingdom come. Your will be done, on earth as it is in heaven" (Matthew 6:9-10 NASB).

On September 23rd, 1857, a lay missionary named Jeremiah Lanphier of the Reformed Protestant Dutch Church in North America started a noon day prayer meeting for business men in New York's Fulton Street. He originally started it because, after he saw how personal prayer powerfully affected him by granting him a renewed strength and assurance of Divine favor on his labors, he wanted others to feel the same way. What started out as a small weekly meeting (only six people showed up for the first meeting) blossomed to over 20 daily meetings at one time by the beginning of the next year—with newspaper reports going out all over the world because of a mighty revival that was taking place. The result was that more than five hundred thousand came to Christ in just one year's time with spontaneous and organized prayer taking place all across the United States. There was no keynote speaker, prominent revivalist or any keen marketing—it was just people gathering together to pray.[1]

The Power of Corporate Prayer

I remember one night in the mid-1990s when I heard on the news that a category four or five hurricane was going to directly hit Puerto Rico. Forecasters were predicting that it might wipe out the entire island. I was greatly concerned for the many pastors and churches I knew who lived there.

Later that night, we had our usual Tuesday night prayer meeting. During the service the Holy Spirit gave me great liberty to pray in faith against the hurricane. After about 45 minutes of intense intercession, the burden suddenly lifted, and we all had an assurance that the storm would miss the island.

The Lord had given me such peace and confidence that the next morning when I turned on the eight o'clock news, I expected to hear that the storm had changed course. To my disappointment, I heard that it was still heading right toward the beautiful island of Puerto Rico. I had to fight confusion and discouragement, wondering if I had really heard from God the night before. Then I realized that I still had a powerful sense of confidence that the Lord had heard and was answering our prayers.

At the end of the newscast, the weatherman came back on and announced that the storm had just changed direction and was heading out to sea. It was going to miss Puerto Rico entirely. I believe that the hurricane's change of course was primarily due to our local church standing in the gap and persevering until we received God's peace concerning this situation. (Of course, I am sure that there were numerous churches in Puerto Rico and beyond praying against this storm as well, but I do believe that God used us in a significant way.)

Even though God is sovereign, He also expects us to exercise our authority through faith so that lives can be saved. This is the kind of prayer He has called us to. This is the level of prayer that alters the destiny of nations.

This reminds me of the Gospel story in which Jesus calmed the storm so that He and His disciples could get to the other side of a lake and preach the Gospel (see Mark 4:35-41). The Church is called to use the prayer of faith to change both the physical and spiritual environment so that the Lord can be glorified through His people.

Kingdom-Centered Prayer

Often when we think of prayer, we think of a person having a quiet devotional time in which the devotee experiences inward renewal and refreshment. King David reiterated time and again that he only found the strength and courage he needed when he *"strengthened himself in the Lord"* (1 Sam. 30:6 NKJV).

However, we also need to move outside of ourselves toward a world in desperate need of prayer. Of all the examples of prayer in the Bible, a disproportionate amount of them have to do with God using an individual to change the destiny of whole nations and empires. A good example of this is when Moses prayed asking God not to destroy the nation of Israel for making a golden calf (see Exod. 32:1-14).

God wants to teach His people the nature and significance of prayer in relation to fulfilling the Cultural Mandate and discipling the nations. Since our world is sick and dying, we are asked by our King to move beyond our own hurts and bruises and to take on the same burden for others that Jesus bore when He walked on earth as a man.

The Spirit of the Sovereign Lord is on Me, because the Lord has anointed Me to preach good news to the poor. He has sent Me to bind up the brokenhearted, to proclaim freedom for the captives and release from darkness for the prisoners, to proclaim the year of the Lord's favor and day of vengeance of our God, to comfort all who mourn, and provide for those who grieve in Zion—to bestow on them a crown of beauty instead of ashes, the oil of gladness instead of mourning, and a garment of praise instead of a spirit of despair . . . (Isaiah 61:1-3 NIV).

Praying for the poor, the brokenhearted, and the prisoners of darkness will not compromise our intimacy with our heavenly Father. Rather, God draws close to those who pray to be sent to the front lines to advance His purposes. In this chapter, we will briefly survey some of the prayers of God's Kingdom warriors so our faith and prayer focus can begin to approach Kingdom proportions for our communities, workplaces, churches, and homes.

Abraham

Abraham was supernaturally called by God to leave his natural family to go to a strange place to receive the promise of an inheritance (see Gen. 12:1-4; Heb. 11:8-9). God told Abraham that, even though he was 99 years old and Sarah's womb was barren, the natural seed from their loins would become a great nation and bless all the families of the earth (see Gen. 17:1-8; Rom. 4:19).

Many of us would have been discouraged by these circumstances, but Abraham was an experienced intercessor with an intimate knowledge of, and friendship with, God (see James 2:23). Scripture recounts that most of his prayers and his time with the Lord had to do with the destiny of the nations and the history of the world.

In Genesis 13:14-18, after a disappointing separation from his nephew Lot, Abram is told to envision the land that God would give to him as an inheritance for his seed, which God said would be as numerous as *"the dust of the earth."* In Genesis 15:1-21, God made a covenant with Abram, promising him that He would make him exceedingly fruitful, the father of many nations, and that kings would come out of his loins. In Genesis 17:15-19, his wife Sarah was also told that she would be the mother of nations and that kings would come from her *"barren womb."*

Through his many years of walking with God, Abraham developed a great compassion for humanity, which resulted in intense intercession for people groups not related to him and his seed. We see one such account of this when he prayed for the deliverance of two cities that God said were about to be destroyed.

Genesis 18:16-33 is a very powerful passage that shows the potential of intercession as Abraham prayed for God to spare Sodom from being destroyed. I doubt there was any one else on the earth who could have penetrated the heart of God in a way that almost changed the course of history for thousands of people. Abraham had such a powerful ability in prayer because he took the time to develop an intimate relationship with God.

Today God is beckoning us to become His intimate friends. When we pray we need to be open to God as He downloads pictures of what He has called us to do to impact our world for future generations. Only when we get to Heaven will we finally realize the full significance of what our prayers have done to change the course of world history.

Jacob

Abraham's grandson Jacob also knew about the power of prayer. Although he knew about the promise of blessing that God had given to his grandfather, it seems Jacob was an unbeliever in his youth, deceiving both his father and older brother into giving him the blessing.[2]

Genesis 28:10-14 illustrates a very powerful encounter that Jacob had with God during which He reconfirmed the covenant that He had made with Abraham. God told Jacob that his seed would be as the dust of the earth and that they would bless all of the families of the earth. Jacob turned his life around, married, and had 12 sons who became a family of 70. Jacob foresaw God's blessing on his family and prayed over each of his sons, prophesying over their destinies before he died (see Gen. 49).

This fascinating story teaches us how even an unconverted, self-centered deceiver can be turned around by one personal encounter with our God. The history of the world was forever changed when Jacob put his head on that stone and allowed God to speak to him and give him a vision about his future.[3] Because of that one experience, Jacob began a journey with God that resulted in his seed multiplying and becoming the nation of Israel, which eventually produced the Messiah, Jesus Christ.

Daniel

The Book of Daniel is one of the greatest Old Testament examples of the power and importance of prayer. In Daniel 9:3-19, this powerful man of God identified with the sins of his nation when he prayed, *"We have sinned and have committed iniquity and have done wickedly and have rebelled."* Even though he was a man of integrity and there is no biblical record of him personally turning away from God, he understood corporate destiny and the importance of godly leaders taking responsibility for others in prayer.

He had a heart for God's Kingdom and even spent weeks fasting over Israel's captivity, even though he was one of the leaders of Persia and most likely very well off financially. His supplication paved the way for God to fulfill the prophecy of Jeremiah in which the Lord brought Israel out of their 70-year captivity (see Dan. 9:2).

During a three-week vegetable fast, Daniel had a visitation from God similar to that of John the Revelator (see Dan. 10:5-10; Rev. 1:12-18). God revealed that his prayer for Israel's deliverance would be answered and showed him some of the things occurring in the spiritual realm between demonic principalities and God's angelic host.[4] We see this illustrated in Daniel 10:20 when an angelic being, Michael, fought with the ruling demonic angel over Persia, called the prince of Persia.[5]

This illustrates that prayer enables God's people to be actively involved in the spiritual warfare taking place between the angelic and demonic hosts. Thus, we can help determine which nations rule the earth and which nations dissipate in earthly power and influence. This is the kind of prayer I want to devote myself to—prayers involving the destiny of nations and empires for thousands of years to come.

There are many other examples of God's people who relied on prayer to combat evil in society. Take time and read the Book of Nehemiah and the Book of Esther. The Bible clearly teaches that the destinies of whole nations are affected by the power of God's people in prayer.

The Prayers of Jesus

The Lord's Prayer (Matthew 6:9-13)

The Lord's Prayer is one of the most compelling passages of Scripture. While most merely recite it, Jesus used it as a template detailing the protocol, purpose, and power of prayer. We have to learn the correct protocol so we can enjoy complete access to God in prayer.

If you had a meeting with the Queen of England, you could not just walk up to her and give her a list of your wants and needs. You would need to be instructed on what to do when you approached her in the palace. You would need to know proper protocol, or it would be a complete waste of time. Our prayers need to have a specific Kingdom purpose and not just express our personal needs. Through prayer we can release His Kingdom power on earth and resist temptation from the evil one.

Each sentence of this model prayer is a category intended to release a particular prayer focus in the order of God's priority for our lives. Let's walk through His prayer step by step so as to grasp its full significance.

Our Father who is in heaven, hallowed be Your name (Matthew 6:9 NASB).

The first order of prayer for the believer is to praise God in the context of covenant relationship with Him. To the world He is God, but to us He is *Father*. We must relate to Him in this context; otherwise we miss His purpose for our relationship. We are to minister to God in praise and adoration before we petition Him for our needs.

Your kingdom come. Your will be done, on earth as it is in heaven (Matthew 6:10 NASB).

Jesus calls us to keep the Cultural Mandate of Genesis 1:28 at the center of our prayer life. Our attitude toward Him and others must be for the good of all human kind. This means that rather than putting individual petitions first, Jesus instructs us to seek first His Kingdom and desire to make the earth reflect Heaven. Too many saints begin with inwardly focused prayers and then wonder why God doesn't answer them. With these two phrases serving as our table-setters for prayer, we can then proceed to our personal petitions.

Give us this day our daily bread (Matthew 6:11 NASB).

Those who follow God's order and protocol for prayer can now expect God's propitious provision. What Jesus is teaching us here is the fact that God will take care of all of our personal needs if we first focus on and pray about releasing His Kingdom will on the earth.

The Lord's Prayer should be taken in the context of the whole chapter. Thus we can better understand why Jesus concluded this chapter by saying that if we put God's Kingdom and His righteousness first, then all our personal needs will be taken care of and we will not be plagued by constant worry (see Matt. 6:33-34).

And forgive us our debts, as we also have forgiven our debtors (Matthew 6:12 NASB).

The most important thing in prayer is to have a correct heart relationship with God. When we put the Kingdom of God first, we are better able to move forward in forgiveness, even in the midst of relational challenges. Desiring what is good regarding His Kingdom (rather than merely seeking to satisfy our own needs and feelings) allows us to enjoy the deepest and most satisfying relationships with others. We will also be able to experience a deeper cleansing of the blood of Christ through forgiving others, thereby advancing God's Kingdom through bringing unity within the Body of Christ.[6]

And do not lead us into temptation, but deliver us from evil... (Matthew 6:13 NASB).

Temptation for those who are Kingdom-focused is broader than lapses in personal morality. As we mature in the Kingdom, we learn that temptations go from just personal moral issues to include having too many ministry options distracting us from doing God's will. We need to resist the temptation to do good works (that aren't God's works), and we need to focus on what God has called us to do.

For example, when I first came to Christ, my biggest temptation may have been issues of the flesh. Now my primary temptation has to do with constantly staying focused on the main items that the Lord puts in front of me. I have to be like a laser beam in regards to what activities I am involved in and what invitations I accept. Any activity outside my primary Kingdom assignment can cause me to miss the mark.

Satan comes as an angel of light, not in a red suit with a pitchfork; therefore, some of my greatest temptations may even come cloaked in religious functions, such as an invitation to minister in a setting that the Lord never assigned to me. The enemy tempts us with various good activities that may actually distract us from God's best.

...For Yours is the kingdom and the power and the glory forever. Amen (Matthew 6:13 NASB).

This prayer both begins and ends with a focus on God and His Kingdom. Jesus seems to be making sure that His disciples understood that the focus of their life and prayers should be the Kingdom of God, not their own needs.

Jesus employed the "sandwich approach," using the main theme as the starting point as well as the conclusion to His model prayer. The first thing we are to pray is for His Kingdom to come and His will to be done. We are to end our prayer by declaring our allegiance to His Kingdom.

Jesus' Prayer for His Followers (John 17:1-26)

In John 16, Jesus told His disciples what was about to happen and concluded by saying, *"These things I have spoken to you, so that in Me you may have peace. In the world you have tribulation, but take courage; I have overcome the world"* (John 16:33 NASB). Then He proceeded to pray for His disciples and all the many believers who would follow after them. His prayer is replete with Kingdom language.

In John 17:2, Jesus started off by stating that the Father had given Him authority over all flesh for the sake of granting eternal life to the elect. Thus His primary concern was utterly selfless. His love for humanity was at the very forefront of all He said and did.

In John 17:6-8, Jesus faithfully discharged the duties of manifesting the Father's name to those whom the Father had given Him. He did this by showing that all that He had on the earth was given to Him by the Father and that He wasn't self-sufficient in His humanity.

Scripture teaches us that we need to live by the Spirit in order to fulfill the will of God on the earth (see Gal. 5:16-17). Zechariah 4:6 says that victory comes, *"...'Not by might nor by power, but by My Spirit,' says the Lord Almighty"* (NIV). Therefore, manifesting the name of God has to do with expressing the person, power, deeds, and will of the Father who has commissioned us.

In John 17:15, Jesus said to the Father, *"My prayer is not that You take them out of the world but that You protect them from the evil one"* (NIV). This amazing verse shows that Kingdom-centered prayer is contrary to the contemporary obsession that many of us have with being rescued out of the world.

Hence, the essence of this Kingdom prayer has to do with the Church being strategically sent forth into the world to engage the culture as salt and light rather than hoping for a divine escape and rescue operation—something that (in natural warfare) only takes place when the soldiers are defeated (see Acts 3:21).

In John 17:21-23, Jesus prayed for unity, which was fulfilled when the Church was legally placed within each of the members of the Godhead—Father, Son, and Holy Spirit—and when the divide between Jew and Gentile was broken at the cross. The Church will never mature as long as individualism is rampant because perfection and maturity will only come through relating both locally and universally to other members of the Church.

John 17:23 says, *"I in them, and You in Me, that they may be perfected in unity, so that the world may know that You sent Me, and have loved them, even as You have loved Me"* (NASB). Irrespective of all the evangelistic strategies that the Church employs, the world will never believe that Jesus was sent by God to be the Savior without purposeful, Kingdom-centered unity.

The Hall of Faith

Hebrews 11:1 says, *"Faith is the substance of things hoped for, the evidence of things not seen."* This verse teaches us that faith to believe God for the impossible first starts in our hearts. Hebrews 11:3 teaches us that through faith God framed or created the universe. We know that God spoke the world into existence in Genesis chapter 1, so He is telling us that faith-filled words have amazing creative power.

Hebrews 11:32-33 speaks of Gideon, Barak, Samson, Jephthah, David, Samuel, and the prophets *"who through faith subdued kingdoms...."* I have no problem with the faith message of earlier decades except that it didn't go far enough. Instead of merely hoping for personal prosperity and healing, we need to understand that we are primarily called to use our faith to subdue kingdoms and *"turn to flight the armies of the aliens,"* as explained in Hebrews 11:34. Rather than focusing on our individual rights, desires, and needs, we must, as Jesus and these heroes of faith have taught us, focus our prayers first on His Kingdom (see Luke 11:2).

Paul's Prayer in Ephesians

In Ephesians 1:9-10, Paul teaches that the ultimate purpose of God is to *"gather together in one all things in Christ."* He follows with a Kingdom prayer for the Church so that this purpose in Christ would be fulfilled.

> *That the God of our Lord Jesus Christ, the Father of glory, may give to you a spirit of wisdom and of revelation in the knowledge of Him. I pray that the eyes of your heart may be enlightened, so that you may know what the hope of His calling is, and what are the riches of the glory of His inheritance in the saints, and what is the surpassing greatness of His power toward us who believe.*

> *These are in accordance with the working of the strength of His might which He brought about in Christ when He raised Him from the dead, and seated Him at His right hand in the heavenly places, far above all rule and authority and power and dominion, and every name that is named, not only in this age, but also in the one to come, and He put all things in subjection under His feet, and gave Him as head over all things to the church, which is His body, the fullness of Him who fills all in all* (Ephesians 1:17-23 NASB).

This powerful prayer shows the connection between the believer and the Risen Lord who alone is above every power and name and ruler in the universe! It is only through the power of the risen Christ that the Church can promote the Kingdom of God in every realm of life.

First Timothy 2:1-4 teaches that corporate prayer and intercession for kings and civic leaders can change the course of history and grant us peace instead of war so that the Gospel can go forth for the glory of God, *"who will have all men to be saved and to come unto the knowledge of the truth."*

THINK ON THIS

These passages should greatly build our faith since they show the incredible relationship between prayer, encounters with God, and our call to reflect God's Kingdom on earth. As we conclude this chapter, we should ponder whether our prayers have been focused just on personal needs or on the Kingdom of God.

Write a personal prayer using the Lord's Prayer as your guide.

Read again how Jesus prayed for His followers in John 17.

Using what you have learned, write a prayer that asks God to send you forth strategically into your area of influence as salt and light.

Make a list of civic leaders you need to begin interceding for. Join with others in your church or prayer group in praying for each one of these men and women. Keep a journal and record the changes you see in your local government as a result of your prayer.

Endnotes

1. Talbot Chambers, *The New York City Noon Prayer Meeting* (Colorado Springs, CO: Campus Renewal Ministries, 2007). It was reprinted with permission from Global Harvest Ministries.

2. In Genesis 25:29-34, Jacob took advantage of his brother Esau's physical hunger and convinced him to sell him his birthright in return for food. In Genesis 27:1-29, he then proceeded to trick his father into giving him the blessing of the firstborn, which belonged

to Esau, by taking advantage of his father's old age and physical blindness.

3. Jacob placing his head on the stone can be seen as a metaphor for a person putting their thoughts on Jesus, who is called the stone in First Peter 2:7.

4. The position of these hierarchies dictated which nation would have ascendancy to global power. Demonic entities position themselves for a time over a nation or continent until angelic hosts resist and remove them as determined by the sovereignty of God.

5. World history teaches us that after Daniel's time, the Persian Empire was conquered by Alexander the Great, who was the leader of Greece. This was several hundred years before Christ was born. From this passage we can surmise that the shift of power and dominance between nations had to do with the positioning of both angelic and demonic beings as they engaged in spiritual warfare.

6. Mark 11:25, John 17:20-23, and First John 1:7 show that God's Kingdom mandate requires the highest levels of trust and covenant because of the intense spiritual warfare launched by satan to divide the Church.

CHAPTER 9
THE ADVANCEMENT OF THE KINGDOM

Jesus and just a small band of disciples started a movement that has become the most powerful in the history of the world. Many different kinds of people with various gifts, personalities, education, rank, and calling have contributed to its phenomenal success. Although the message never changes, we must note that God employs a wide variety of methods to advance His Kingdom here on the earth.

As we study His Word and Church history, we find that God is a lot more flexible in His methods than we may have originally thought. For example, in the early 1550s, the great theologian, John Calvin, wrote a systematic theological treatise called *The Institutes of the Christian Religion* that was read by millions of Christians. He also founded Geneva Academy, the first Protestant university that subsequently trained thousands of students for the ministry and began the vast Reformed Church movement that still exists today. His starting point was God's sovereignty, and he emphasized doctrine and proper church government as the keys for reformation.

Martin Luther, the Catholic monk who started the Protestant Reformation by hanging his 95 Theses on the door of the Castle Church in Wittenberg, Germany, emphasized justification by faith. Erasmus didn't agree with Luther's break from the Catholic church and tried to reform the Roman Catholic church from within, teaching that education was the key to reform.

Savonarola, a 15th-century Catholic priest, used his great abilities as a preacher to denounce the abuses in the church and was executed after he denounced Pope Alexander VI. When Peter Waldo, a wealthy merchant of Lyons, was converted, he gave away his worldly possessions and went about preaching the Gospel. He subsequently organized a large movement of prophetic evangelists who were excommunicated from the Church in 1184 by Pope Lucius III.

Count Zinzendorf, an 18th-century Lutheran nobleman, allowed a company of Moravian refugees to settle on his estate in Berthelsdorf. These new settlers called their settlement "Herrnhut," which means "The Lord's Watch." After attending a powerful communion service in Herrnhut in 1727, Zinzendorf felt the Lord had called him to renew the Moravian movement started a few centuries earlier by John Huss. Both Zinzendorf and John Wesley, the 18th-century revivalist who founded Methodism, were both administrative geniuses who decentralized authority and spread the Gospel using small groups of believers.

The 16th-century Scottish preacher John Knox, the great 19th-century American revivalist Charles Finney, and the powerful English pastor Charles Spurgeon all preached primarily inside churches. George Whitfield, perhaps the most prominent revivalist in England and America during the 18th century, spoke primarily outside in open fields.

Abraham Kuyper was an ideological coalition builder. Philip Jacob Spener, an 18th-century Lutheran minister, taught intimacy with God and brought the pietistic movement to the Lutheran Church.

The founder of the Quakers, George Fox, focused on the "inner light," while St. Augustine worked toward building the City of God.

The Anabaptists taught pacifism and the separation between church and state. The Puritans, who fled England and settled in the New World because of religious persecution, applied the Bible to all areas of life in order to bring about cultural transformation.

C.S. Lewis used his pen to author the famous series, *The Chronicles of Narnia,* and the most influential Christian book of the 20th century, *Mere Christianity.* Mel Gibson used a movie screen to portray *The Passion of the Christ.*

In the first-century Church, Peter emphasized power. John emphasized love. Paul emphasized doctrine. Barnabas emphasized unity in the Church. Paul's epistle to the Philippians emphasized the community of faith, and his epistle to the Colossians emphasized the cosmic Christ as the head over all creation.

The purpose of this chapter is not to emphasize any one way or to comprehensively cover every method, but to examine some of the macro themes of Scripture regarding how the Kingdom of God is advertised and effectively advanced to fulfill the Cultural Commission.

Our Love

In John 13:35, Jesus told His disciples, *"By this all men will know that you are My disciples, if you have love for one another"* (NASB). Love is by far the most powerful force in the universe. First John 4:8 says that *"God is love."* If truth is the message, love is the messenger. People don't care how much you know until they know how much you care. I have seen hard-hearted people melt like wax before the white-hot flames of love. The Bible tells us in First Corinthians 13:8 that spiritual gifts will fail, cease, or vanish, but love will never fail.

First Corinthians 13:13 says that between faith, hope, and love, the greatest is love. Tradition has it that when John the beloved apostle was old, his disciples would practically carry him into a meeting, and he would just say, "Little children, love one another."

I heard a preacher tell how he became discouraged when he found out that only a few members of his congregation were living out the truths he was teaching. One Sunday, he stood up to preach and out of this frustration all that came out of his mouth was, "Love one another." Then he sat down and waited in silence for 45 minutes. People just stared at him, thinking it was a joke. But he never got up from his seat. The next week he did the same thing, and the week after that.

Finally a man stood up and said, "I know what the pastor is trying to get us to do—he wants us to *really* love one another." So he asked the person next to him how he was doing and what his needs were. Another person gave money to someone he knew was in need. Still another began to pray for the person next to him. On and on this went until a great revival broke out in the church.

Sometimes our greatest challenge is that we think we need more Bible knowledge. The truth is that we already have more knowledge than the greatest preachers of the early Church, yet we experience far fewer results. After reading the first six chapters of the Book of Acts, I realized that if I were to go back to the first-century Church, I wouldn't even qualify as a home group leader.

The deacons of the early Church had more power than the apostolic leaders alive today (see Acts 6–8). They didn't study healing; they just went out in the streets and laid hands on the sick. They didn't spend endless years studying systematic theology; they put the Word into practice, caring for the widows, orphans, and the poor (see James 1:27). The story of the Church is called "The Book of Acts"—not "the book of truths."

Experience has taught me that I learn more by doing than by just reading about how something is done. What I read always makes more sense when it is something that I have actually experienced. Unused knowledge is usually lost very quickly. For example, most people forget 90 percent of the sermon they hear on Sunday within a few hours if they do not find a way to apply it in their real lives. In comparison, the teacher or preacher has had to process and apply the information that he has studied in order to present it to others.

Two days after 9/11, most of my fellow New Yorkers were incited against Islam. However, I saw it as an opportunity to begin to tear down the walls between Christians and Muslims in my community. I put on my clergy collar and went first to one and then to a second mosque located within close proximity of my house.

I respectfully took my shoes off and went inside during their worship service. I was immediately escorted into the office of the head imam and asked why I was there. I gave them my business card, told them I was a community leader, and said I was willing to help them if they needed me. I explained that I wanted them to know that I wasn't blaming all Muslims for what had happened and that I believed I was to extend love and friendship to them.

As soon as I finished speaking, the leaders of both mosques started weeping and began to hug me. To this day I don't know the total impact this had on them, but I know it sowed the seeds of love that may have stopped them from participating in a future terrorist attack and may have instead resulted in their eventual salvation. It wasn't a debate on doctrine that touched them—it was love.

At the end of this chapter is a powerful testimony from one of the members of our church that saliently illustrates the essence of love.

Our Hope

Hope is probably the most underrated attribute of God. But it is the fuel that keeps our engines going and the motivation that pushes us through the tests of life. It is perhaps the most efficacious advertisement for the advancement of the Kingdom of God. It takes what we anticipate in the future and makes it a present reality. In Titus 2:13, our final redemption is called *"the blessed hope."* Optimism, a symptom of hope, repels those great killers of faith, hope, and love: pessimism and cynicism.

A Christian's optimism is not based on myth but on the reality of His blessed hope. We have this hope because we know the end of the book—Christ's ultimate triumph over evil. But the Bible's major theme, which is carefully woven throughout all its books, is the triumph of the Kingdom of God over the kingdom of darkness. Our hope for victory is based on the promise of God that He is a *very present help in trouble* (Ps. 46:1). Hope is the substance of faith and the carrier of the hidden title deed that provides the evidence of things not seen (see Heb. 11:1).

Hope is Christianity's greatest witness, the entrée to conversation and the bridge to a person's felt needs and hidden wants (see 1 Pet. 3:15). Non-Christians should desire our hope and crave our optimism. The healthy should be willing to die for it, the sick should be willing to be healed by it, and the rich should be willing to give all away for it (see John 21:18; Prov. 17:22; Matt. 13:45-46).

We may not have the talent for fame or the gifts to stand before the great, but we can all have hope because of the love of God in our hearts (see 1 Tim. 5:5). Most of God's army is made up of people without an impressive resumé regarding financial portfolios, fame, or power so that God will get the glory (see 1 Cor. 1:26-27). Truly His plan is for ordinary people to do extraordinary things through the blessed hope that the Gospel gives us.

Just this past week, I learned that a shy, quiet church member has started a small group at her job. The group meets once a week during their lunch break. She excitedly shared how God was using her to lead fellow workers to Christ and to pray for divine healings. One person's cancer even disappeared. This woman is too shy to even give her testimony in front of our congregation, yet God is using her to do awesome things for His Kingdom in her workplace. Her great hope in the power of the Gospel has led her to do extraordinary things and to advance His Kingdom in her area of influence.

Our Service

Our service to others dignifies them, sanctifies the concept of human life, and affirms a person's worth (like when a nurse diligently cares for the dying and needy in the hospital). Jesus brought service to a whole new level when He stooped down to wash the feet of His disciples (see John 13). This was significant because in Greco-Roman culture only slaves did the dirty work and hard labor.

Actions speak so loudly that sometimes people don't hear what we are saying. Before we declare the Gospel to our community, we must incarnate the Gospel by feeding the hungry, watering the thirsty, housing the homeless, clothing the naked, visiting the prisoners, healing the sick, and empowering the feeble (see Matt. 25:31-46).

Though Christians are already righteous by their position, service gives us favor. We are saved by God. But are we respected by man?

When Mother Teresa spoke at the National Prayer Breakfast in 1994, she strongly chastised pro-choice people for their stance on abortion. A reporter later asked then-President Clinton, a known pro-choice advocate, what he had thought about Mother Teresa's words, and he replied, "How can anyone argue with a life so well-lived?"[1]

My wife and I have taken this principle to heart and have ministered to tens of thousands of at-risk children since 1981. Then when the time came to lead the fight against same-sex marriage in our city, we had already earned a place of respect because of the service we had freely given to our community.

Marvin Olasky's book, *Compassionate Conservatism,* became one of the major campaign themes of George W. Bush during his first term as president. The fact that the general populace needed a marketing spin to connect compassion with conservatism is the greatest tragedy of the 20th century. The fact that Christians have been known more for Bible-thumping than foot washing and for denunciation rather than community participation is something the evangelical Church must remedy if we are going to be culturally relevant in America.

James 2:20-26 reminds us that just as the body without the spirit is dead, so faith without works is dead. Service is to the

Gospel what a notary stamp is to a document—it authenticates our faith. Gandhi is alleged to have said, "I would have become a Christian if it weren't for Christians."

There have been some signs of hope that the Church is finally beginning to understand the need to serve humanity. Chuck Colson globally leads the way in prison reform. World Vision, the Salvation Army, and other Christian aid organizations were an enormous help to the Indonesian victims of the 2004 tsunami. The Body of Christ has also led the charge in disaster relief and rebuilding efforts in New Orleans in the aftermath of Hurricane Katrina.

Evangelical organizations are doing more than any others for the AIDS pandemic in Africa, the slave trade in the Sudan, and the sex slave trade of young girls in Asia. Truly the world is not looking for another great preacher, but for a Church of great ministers. Even so, Lord, work this into the heart of Your people (see Phil. 2:12-13).

Jesus instructed us in Matthew 5:16, *"Let your light shine before men that they may see your good deeds and glorify your Father in heaven"* (NIV). This means that all saints are called by God to make a difference by serving fellow humanity as we have the opportunity. Just doing acts of kindness like shoveling snow for the elderly, shopping for the disabled, and baby-sitting for single moms may be enough to win the hearts of many people for the Kingdom.

Our Doctrine

Between the anti-intellectual posture of evangelicals during the 1900s and the postmodern culture since the 1970s, doctrine has been downplayed and has even received a bad name in some church cultures. By doctrine I mean a systematic understanding of the essentials of the faith—something the Scriptures admonish us to each have (see Heb. 5:12–6:3). In Second Timothy 2:15, God commands us to study the Word so that we are *"correctly analyzing and accurately dividing [rightly handling and skillfully teaching] the Word of Truth"* (AMP).

It is not that every Christian should be a theologian, but they should at least understand all the essentials of the faith. They must be able to articulate to others what they believe and why they believe it (see 1 Pet. 3:15). In First Corinthians 3:1-2, Paul encourages all saints to be able to receive the wisdom of God instead of just the milk of the Word. I believe every preacher and teacher of the Gospel should be a theologian (one who, like Apollos in Acts 18:24, is competent in the Scriptures) and not just an able orator, because James 3:1 warns that we who teach will receive stricter judgment.

Romans, Ephesians, Colossians, and Hebrews are all about systematic doctrine. Much of Exodus, Leviticus, Numbers, and Deuteronomy are about laws, precepts, and doctrine. Job teaches God-centered philosophy, and Psalm 119 is devoted to the law/word of Jehovah. Jude 3 teaches us to *"contend for the faith that was once for all entrusted to the saints"* (NIV).

How can we contend for something if we don't have a systematic belief system? When telling Timothy how to emulate him, Paul mentioned doctrine first on the list of his key attributes (along with his *"manner of life, purpose, faith, longsuffering, charity, patience"*) and warned of a time coming when folks would not *"endure sound doctrine"* (2 Tim. 3:10; 4:3).

Doctrine crystallizes what we feel, intuit, and read about God. It systematically arranges our thoughts and beliefs into one coherent narrative and enables us to skillfully communicate our faith according to the topic and questions at hand. In John 18:37-38, Jesus knew and communicated what He believed to the unbelieving Pilate.

Doctrine is absolutely necessary to both defend and propagate the truth. Paul told Titus that we convince the gainsayers with sound doctrine (see Titus 1:9). He also instructed Timothy to gently teach those who opposed him so that they could be released from the captivity of satan and led to the "knowledge of the truth" (2 Tim. 2:25-26 NIV).

Christians have the unique ability to give answers that unlock the mysteries of life. We need to take advantage of this, especially in regards to applying the biblical worldview to current events and public policy. Those ready to give an answer for the hope that is in them will have a continual flow of people coming to them because of the universal hunger in this world for truth.

I have had hundreds of conversations over the years with non-Christians who wanted answers regarding the problem of evil, the existence of God, the love of God, prayer, and the judgment to come. I was able to give a cogent response to these questions, which enabled me to lead many of these people to faith in Christ. If all I had was spirituality without systematic knowledge of the Scriptures, then many of these people may have remained in their state of doubt toward God.

Our Tradition

Religious traditions can bring stability to family and society. Our families need to be surrounded by Christian emblems, signs, and traditions that mark them as God's distinct and holy people. Numerous passages in the New Testament are allegedly part of the traditions handed down directly from Jesus and the original 12 apostles.[2]

Unfortunately, when the Pentecostals were put out of the mainline Protestant denominations in the early 20th century, tradition went out the window in favor of being led by the Holy Spirit. This resulted in many churches throwing the baby out with the bathwater. The mainline denominations have many good traditions that can and should be kept for the good of all Christian congregations.

For example, our church began having Confirmation classes a few years ago because we realized that all children need a "rite of passage" that shows their transition into adulthood. Without these traditions, there is a vacuum that causes Christian families to unwittingly utilize familiar cultural benchmarks instead. For boys it seems to be getting a driver's license, and for girls it seems to be the "sweet 16" birthday party.

We were able to garner ideas from the Roman Catholic and Lutheran churches for these classes, which have proven to be powerful benchmarks in the lives of our young people. They attend classes for two years, starting with the sixth grade. The classes culminate with a graduation ceremony in which each child receives a ring from their parents that involves making a vow of chastity until they get married. One of my sons told me that these classes and this ring even helped keep him from falling into sin while in high school.

In the Old Testament, the Jews celebrated three major feasts every year: the Feast of Passover, the Feast of Weeks or Pentecost, and the Feast of Tabernacles (see Deut. 16:16). These feasts became part of a tradition that served to continually instruct the generations of Jewish young people in the faith and illustrated the difference between Israel and the unbelieving world. God gave us these traditions to remind us of His faithfulness and His promises. In the New Testament, the apostle Paul saw the importance of recognizing these feasts (see Acts 20:16).

The Fourth Commandment teaches God's covenant community to set aside one day per week to abstain from work and to worship God (see Exod. 20:8). The Church changed it from the seventh day to the first day of the week to commemorate the day of new beginnings when Jesus rose from the dead (see Matt. 28:1-6; 1 Cor. 16:2; Rev. 1:10).

The distinct Christian seasons of Christmas, Lent, and Resurrection Day (Easter), plus the traditions of water baptism, baby dedication, Sunday school, catechism training, confirmation, holy communion, and family devotions are all meant to teach and confirm believers and to be a witness of the Christian faith to unbelievers (see 1 Cor. 11:26).

Just as Paul handed down the traditions to his disciples, children growing up in Christian homes have a litany of traditions that embody and confirm their faith so that, as they mature, they will not apostatize or renounce their faith when faced with worldly influences and challenges.

If a local congregation just honored each of these distinct times of the year, it would be a great lesson in itself for all participants. For example, water baptism speaks about a believer identifying themselves with the death, burial, and resurrection of Christ and provides a great opportunity for a pastor to teach the essentials of the Gospel and the vicarious nature of the cross of Christ (see Rom. 6:1-7).

Celebrating Christmas is a great opportunity for explaining how God reached out to us by sending His Son as a human being so that He might redeem us from our sins and become a bridge between humans and God. Lent is a great way for the Church to commemorate the 40 days before Good Friday and to teach fasting, prayer, and repentance. Holy communion connects Christians with God through the physical emblems of His grace.

Catechisms are truths put together in the form of questions replete with scriptural answers that are fantastic for helping children understand the Bible as well as all the essential doctrines of the faith. *Catechism* comes from the word *catechize,* which means to train. Proverbs 22:6 instructs us to *"Train a child in the way he should go, and when he is old he will not turn from it"* (NIV). What better way is there to ensure the advancement of God's Kingdom into the next generation?

The Power of God

Before Jesus ascended to the Father, He told His disciples to go into all the world and preach the good news to all creation. He promised them that *"signs shall follow them that believe"* (Mark 16:15-18). After His ascension, the Bible says, *"Then the disciples went out and preached everywhere, and the Lord worked with them and confirmed His word by the signs that accompanied it"* (Mark 16:20 NIV).

Numerous other Bible passages relate how God demonstrates His power and bears personal witness to the resurrection of Christ by performing great miracles and answers to prayer. History also speaks of God using believers to manifest divine healing from the first century to the present. The great Church father Augustine is even said to have had a healing ministry.[3] Romans 9:17 says that God demonstrated His great power in delivering Israel out of Egypt so His name might be known in all the earth.

In John 10, Jesus dealt with the unbelief of the Jews, challenging them by saying:

If I am not doing the works [performing the deeds] of My Father, then do not believe Me [do not adhere to Me and trust Me and rely on Me]. But if I do them, even though you do not believe Me or have faith in Me, [at least] believe the works and have faith in what I do, in order that you may know and understand [clearly] that the Father is in Me, and I am in the Father [One with Him] (John 10:37-38 AMP).

In Mark 2:10, Jesus healed a paralytic man to prove that He can forgive sins. In John 1:47-51, He moved in a word of knowledge to convince Nathaniel to believe that He was the Messiah (see also 1 Cor. 12:8). Both Nicodemus in John 3:1-21 and the blind man whom Jesus healed in John 9 knew that He was sent from God because of the miracles He performed. In John 4:7-40, the woman at the well repented because Jesus revealed the secrets of her heart.

The whole city of Samaria gave heed to the Gospel because they saw the miracles that Philip performed in Acts 8:4-7. The lame man whom Peter healed at the gate of the temple opened a door for him to preach to multitudes in Acts 3:1-12. God gave testimony to the Gospel when He performed signs and wonders by the hands of Paul in Acts 14:3.

The town of Ephesus was shaken because demons testified of Jesus and Paul when they beat up seven unbelievers during an attempted exorcism in Acts 19:13-19. The whole island of Malta was shaken by the power of God when God protected Paul from the bite of a poisonous snake and healed the father of the island's chief official as recorded in Acts 28:1-10.

Power encounters such as these continue to provide a global witness to the Gospel today. Tetsunao Yamamori records the rapid spread of Christianity in contemporary China in his book *Witnesses to Power*.

In Chinese folk religion, sickness is caused by evil spirits the gods sent to punish immoral deeds. When Christianity is introduced in the countryside, people measure its validity on its ability to deliver miracles. If the God of the Christian faith performs miracles that confer benefits on his followers, people are inclined to replace their own deities with this new God. As a result, signs and wonders are commonly found among them and many people turn to Christianity because they experience a physical deliverance from illness or affliction.[4]

On the life of Granny Jie, Tetsunao Yamamori writes:

She had a vision in the 1950's about the coming persecution and felt called of God to the ministry. Afterward she became the pastor of Zhaoxian Gospel Hall. She developed a healing ministry and at the age of 95 she was able to hear, see and preach. She is seldom sick. Whenever she is ill, she always says, "Lord Jesus will heal me." Her confidence is rooted in experience. Many people have been healed following her prayers. Her daily prayer regiment starts at 5 A.M., and every evening from 8 to 8:45 she kneels in prayer. She has been kneeling in prayer for so many years that she has developed a thick callus on her knees. Granny Jie has never taken a day off from the church; she receives no church salary but trusts God for all her needs.[5]

While in China in the spring of 2005, I spent time with members of the house church movement who verified stories like these in their own circles. I heard that in many villages the communists will call for the Christians to pray for them and their families if any are taken with an illness. Divine healing seems to be one of the main evangels of the Gospel in China.

A Nigerian evangelist friend of mine, Victor Emineke, told me that one of the main reasons why Christianity is displacing Islam in Nigeria and many parts of North Africa is because of signs and wonders. A Christian evangelist will go to a town dominated by Islam and hold a public meeting calling for the person with the worst sickness to come forward for prayer.

The evangelist then challenges the head imam to heal the sick person. After the imam either refuses to pray or fails in his attempt, the Christian then proceeds to pray and the person is miraculously healed. Often the head imam and the whole community will receive Christ and convert the mosque into a church.

In my own church, we have seen numerous people receive healing after prayers of faith. One such instance was a man who came to our church dying of AIDS in 1985. He showed me numerous lesions on his tongue and said that he was losing weight and was continually tired. I told him that in the same way he received Christ for forgiveness of sins he could now receive Him as his healer.

He asked Jesus to heal him, and within a matter of days, all of his symptoms left, including the lesions on his tongue. God also took away his homosexuality, and he has since married and has a lovely wife and four beautiful children. The family of the bride insisted that he provide medical documentation to prove that AIDS was no longer in his blood. He submitted and all of the tests showed that he had no trace of AIDS. Unfortunately, his younger brother chose not to repent of homosexuality and died of AIDS a few years later.

I met another young man in his late 20s who had been diagnosed with testicular cancer. Within one year he went from being a robust, muscle-bound, 220-pound man to being 120 pounds with skin that had turned pale yellow. He was given less than six months to live. He told me that one of the elders of his church told him to prepare for his funeral.

I invited him to join a class that I was teaching from Luke 9:1 and Luke 10:17-19 on the authority God gave to all believers. He came and lay down on the front pew while I preached on divine healing (using passages from Isaiah 53:4-5; Matthew 8:16-17; and First Peter 2:24). After a few weeks I had him live with my family so that we could constantly read healing Scriptures to him and bathe him with faith-filled prayers. A doctor's checkup later confirmed that the cancer was gone. He has been married for over 20 years and has four healthy children at the writing of this book.

There are many stories like this that I could give about divine healing in our church, but suffice it to say, it is a present reality and one of God's methods for proving the resurrection of Christ and the reality of His Kingdom (see Matt. 12:28).

As we conclude this chapter, we need to remind ourselves of the limitless methods that God has used throughout Church history to spread the Gospel and advertise His Kingdom. We need to understand the power of faith, hope, and love, and why it is important that our actions correspond to our faith. We also need to understand the importance of solid, biblical doctrine and why it is especially important for us to embrace it in our postmodern culture. Finally, we should ask ourselves if we believe God still does miracles today to prove the resurrection of Christ and advance His Kingdom. If we do, then signs and wonders should follow us as we faithfully seek to fulfill the Great Commission.

THINK ON THIS

Complete the following power statements gleaned from this chapter:

In John 13:35, Jesus told His disciples, "By this all men will know that you are My disciples, if _____

_____."

If truth is the message, _____ is the messenger.

People don't care how much you know until they know
_____.

_____ is Christianity's greatest witness,
the _____ to conversation, and the
_____ to a person's felt needs and hidden wants (see
1 Pet. 3:15).

_____ speak so loudly that sometimes people
don't hear what we are saying.

When Mother Teresa spoke at a prayer breakfast chastising
pro-choice people for their stance on abortion, President Clinton said, "It's hard to argue with a _____."

Christian homes have a litany of traditions that
_____ and _____ their faith so that,
as they mature, they will not apostatize or renounce their faith
when faced with worldly influences and challenges.

Do you believe God still does miracles today? Why?

Take a moment and read the following testimony of a person I
know. It saliently illustrates the essence of love—the laying down
of one life for another person's life.

I was packing up the sheets and towels I was planning on bringing to college when Nicole showed me the ominous bruise on
her leg. It's probably from too much swimming, I thought, and
we decided it was nothing. I would later think back to that moment. We had such naïve and innocuous impressions of the
pernicious bruise, because of course, there was nothing wrong
with a healthy, beautiful 23-year-old.

It was my first week of college when my mother called me to
tell me my sister was diagnosed with Chronic Myelogeneous
Leukemia. Most of the details of that day and the days and
weeks that followed still remain an ominous blur. I do remember waiting to find out the results of testing to determine if I
could be a bone marrow donor for her transplant. A bone marrow transplant was her only slim chance for survival. Six days

later the oncologists at Sloan Kettering Memorial Hospital called us to report that my genetic material resembled my sister's almost as closely as if we were identical twins.

I had always looked up to my sister—her being five years older and having the five more inches in height that I always wanted to have. Even though we looked at the world quite differently, I had always had the sense, sharing funnel cakes on the beach as kids or riding on the handlebars of her bike, that we were somehow really similar. Now our genetic similarity had the chance to save her life.

On the day of the transplant, my sister looked weak but hopeful. The chemotherapy had already caused her to lose her hair and her skin was the color of egg drop soup. When the nurse came to lead me into the operating room, we approached the two enormous metal doors in front of us, and I felt like I was walking in the back of Key Food toward the big metal door where the butcher prepares London broil and packages flank steaks. When the doors swung open and I stepped inside, it was cold inside the operating room. I shivered under my hospital gown and whispered to the nurse, "...I'm scared." "I understand, sweetie," the nurse said as she led me to the operating table, still holding my hand.

When I lay down on the table, the cold chill of the metal touched my bare back and I felt like the animal held down at the veterinary office that urinates on the examination table out of sheer terror. I felt a horrible vulnerability—one that I would recognize later in clients with a quiet empathy. The nurse touched me on the head now as if to calm me down. I waited a few minutes looking around at the lights and the instruments, just talking to God in my head. I was a neophyte patient, never having broken a bone or gotten a stitch before. I had never even had a cavity. In the next few minutes the anesthesiologist began to prepare my hand. She was aged with wrinkly fingers, and I wondered who of the two of us would die first.

The voices in the room began to become obscured as if everyone all at once was talking into an inflated balloon. The operating room light got so bright that I closed my eyes but I could still see it through my eyelids. I heard the nurse ask, "Can you hear me, Danielle?" and I tried to answer her, but it felt like a heavy billow of smoke covered my body and I don't think any words came out of my mouth.

When I opened my eyes next, I saw bodies all around me on gurneys throughout the recovery room. A nurse walking in between me and the sleeping body next to me passed close enough for me to reach her with my hand. She startled a bit and then looked down at me. She couldn't understand what I was asking at first. "What's that?" she asked me the second time. She leaned down closer to my mouth this time. I spoke as loudly as I could, "Did they get enough?" I said.

She smiled and said she would ask my nurse, but I didn't let go of her hand. She looked down at me again. "Did they get enough?" I repeated and I squeezed her as hard as I could. She shook her hand out of mine before walking over to a high counter at the entrance to the room. It was a far different experience than when I entered the operating room. I wasn't scared anymore. I was determined. She finally came back and said, "Yes, dear, they got enough." I collapsed back into a sweet sleep. Now it would be OK for me to die.

That day, all that I could do to save my sister's life, I had done. The weeks that followed for her were horribly sad and painful, and there were many days I wanted to run out of the hospital room and never return. The pain, vomiting, delirium—it all hung so heavy, it felt like all the air was being sucked out of the room by the tubes, machines, and catheters. I sometimes wondered if it was medicine or science fiction. But many nights when my sister was resting in her bed, and I was breathless under isolation gear, I would just take her hand, the way the nurse had taken mine.

Long before I ever studied a word of psychology, I understood the profound experience of using myself as the tool to help another. In my sister's case it was a success, but on the 11th floor at Sloan Kettering we made many friends in those months for whom it was not. Survival was just the beginning of the labored, existential musings that would besiege my thoughts. Fortunately, the experience caused me to reflect on myself and my life in a way that allowed me to consider what was meaningful to me.

We celebrate each year on March 14, the day of the bone marrow transplant. We remember the secret horrors of that cancer and the slow triumphant victory that began in fear and ended in freedom. Somehow, without many words we understand the special significance of our similarities—not just of both loving the ocean and swimming the waves, but also of sharing the same DNA as adults. While we have never spent much time talking about that incredible bond, I hold very dear to me the gift my sister gave me on that first anniversary—a package of lifesavers.

— Danielle Magaldi Dopman

Endnotes

1. "Mother Teresa & Bill Clinton," http://md4jc.blogspot.com/2008/06/mother-teresa-bill-clinton.html

2. Passages like First Timothy 3:16, First Corinthians 15:3-8, Philippians 2:6-11, Acts 20:35, and Second Timothy 2:11-13 were repeated in many of the first-century churches and became part of Scripture.

3. For more information on the history of divine healing in the Church, read *Healing and Christianity* by Morton Kelsey, or *Quenching the Spirit* by William DeArteaga.

4. Tetsunao Yamamori and Kim-kwong Chan, *Witnesses to Power: Stories of God's Quiet Work in a Changing China* (Paternoster, 2002), 42-43.

5. *Ibid.*, 8-12.

CHAPTER 10
THE CLASH OF WORLDVIEWS

Wherever truth is, its false counterpart is not far away. It is axiomatic that anything real always has a counterfeit. There are counterfeit dollar bills and synthetic ways to build muscle with steroids. There is true love, which is based on covenant, and there is counterfeit love based on feelings and self-gratification. It is no different in the Kingdom of God.

In First Kings 22:1-28, we even see that the word of the Lord can be counterfeited. The king of Israel had gathered about 400 prophets together so that he could know the mind of the Lord regarding the outcome of a war with Syria. After these prophets prophesied of victory, King Jehoshaphat (king of Judah) asked if there was a true prophet of Jehovah that he could hear from.

When Micaiah came he told them that the Lord had allowed a lying spirit to speak through the other prophets and that instead of victory the people of Israel would be scattered once their leader was dead. In this instance, both Micaiah and the 400 prophets prophesied in the name of the Lord—but only Micaiah was really speaking from God.

The apostle Paul warned Timothy about false teachers and the false doctrines that they teach:

As I urged you when I went into Macedonia, stay there in Ephesus so that you may command certain men not to teach false

169

doctrines any longer nor to devote themselves to myths and end-less genealogies. These promote controversies rather than God's work—which is by faith (1 Timothy 1:3-4 NIV).

Then in chapter 4, he further warned *"that in later times some will abandon the faith and will follow deceiving spirits and things taught by demons"* (1 Tim. 4:1 NIV). Paul charged this young pastor to:

Guard what has been entrusted to your care. Turn away from godless chatter and the opposing ideas of what is falsely called knowledge, which some have professed and in so doing have wandered from the faith . . . (1 Timothy 6:20-21 NIV).

Then Paul told Timothy how to handle those who held an opposing worldview.

Don't have anything to do with foolish and stupid arguments, because you know they produce quarrels. And the Lord's servant must not quarrel; instead, he must be kind to everyone, able to teach, not resentful. Those who oppose him he must gently instruct, in the hope that God will grant them repentance leading them to a knowledge of the truth, and that they will come to their senses and escape from the trap of the devil, who has taken them captive to do his will (2 Timothy 2:23-26 NIV).

Paul also warned about false angelic appearances in Galatians 1:8: *"But even if we, or an angel from heaven, should preach to you a gospel contrary to what we have preached to you, he is to be accursed"* (NASB).

Deuteronomy 13:1-5 teaches us that God allows false prophets, replete with signs and wonders in their repertoire, to be on the earth as a test to see if people will turn away from the one true God. Second Thessalonians 2:9-11 teaches that the enemy's representatives will display all kinds of counterfeit miracles, signs, and wonders, causing some to refuse to love the truth. Thus God allows strong delusions involving supernatural experiences to see if people will choose to believe a lie instead of the truth.

This is why understanding and knowledge of biblical doctrine and theology along with a working knowledge of the creeds and councils of the first six centuries are vital for Christians who want to remain pure. For those wanting an overview of these creeds and councils, read *Church History in Plain Language* by Bruce Shelley, *The Church in History* by B.K. Kuiper, and *History of the Christian Church* by Philip Schaff.

One thing deceivers have in common is that they propagate error along with their counterfeit supernatural abilities. For example, a cult like Christian Science or Mormonism might counterfeit a physical healing, but then capitalize on the vulnerability of a person to promote the false teachings and doctrines of those particular cults.

Christians are warned to scrutinize supernatural experiences as not all visions and visitations are from the Lord. For example, in 1827 Joseph Smith, a resident of Palmyra, New York, said that the angel Moroni appeared to him and directed him to a stone box with golden plates that contained the true Bible. In 1830 he published *The Book of Mormon* and started the Mormon Church. Among other things, Mormonism erroneously teaches that America's beginnings date back to those dispersed from the ancient Tower of Babel, that Jesus was Michael the angel (thus a created being and not God from eternity), and that polygamy is an acceptable practice.

Although polygamy seemed to be an acceptable practice in the Old Testament, the original template that God laid out for marriage in Genesis 2:24 was between one man and one woman. Another example of this in the Old Testament is in Deuteronomy 17:17, which forbids Israelite kings from "multiply[ing] wives to himself." The New Testament seemed to point back to the stated Genesis model of monogamy when it included in the qualifications for church elders and deacons that they should be "the husband of one wife" (1 Tim. 3:2,12).

Even though Mormons claim to be a branch of Christianity, *The Book of Mormon* contradicts Scripture, which indicates that Mormonism is a cult.

A man or woman of God must know Scripture in order to discern such deception:

All Scripture is God-breathed and is useful for teaching, rebuking, correcting and training in righteousness, so that the man of God may be thoroughly equipped for every good work (2 Timothy 3:16-17 NIV).

Satan is a master counterfeiter because he is not capable of creating anything new. He can only pervert what has already been created. Paul warned us to be careful so that we are not deceived by his cunning like Eve was in the Garden of Eden (see 2 Cor. 11:3-4). The crafty serpent perverted what God told Adam and planted seeds of doubt in the mind of Eve (see Gen. 3:1-7).

In the devil's attempt to entice Jesus in the wilderness, he again perverted God's words. But Jesus remained victorious because He knew the Word and used the truth to send the enemy away in Matthew 4:1-11.

This enemy not only brings individual deception, but he has set up systems of deceit that have captivated whole cultures and nations. For example, secular humanism, which is defined as a religion by many, has captivated the public school systems of Western Europe and North America. Islamic Fundamentalism has succeeded in officially enacting Sharia law by integrating it into the governments of the Middle East and in some of the towns in Europe. The Fascist ideals enacted in Nazi Germany by Hitler were based on his book *Mein Kampf* and the belief in ethnic cleansing for the good of the whole.

Any worldview that does not match up with Kingdom principles will eventually fail, but we must be wise as serpents while gentle as doves in convincingly and effectively presenting the Kingdom worldview (see Matt. 10:16). We need to know what we believe and what the counterfeit looks like, and we need to be prepared to skillfully counter each counterfeit belief system. To do this we must understand what makes a belief system work and how the counterfeits miss the mark.

Consistent, Cohesive, Comprehensive

For any belief system to be effective, it must be consistent, cohesive, and comprehensive. In order to be able to quickly identify the counterfeits of the enemy, we must first understand the Kingdom worldview in light of these three "C's." When we know the truth, it will not only set us free from bondage to sin, but it will also protect us from being deceived by the lies of any other worldview system. In order to effectively counteract a counterfeit, we must be able to convincingly present our worldview and systematically explain our belief system and how it fulfills these three "C's."

Consistent

Consistent means that the system is reasonably or logically harmonious, able to maintain a particular standard, and free of contradiction. Consistency also implies reliability, steadfastness, and dependability. It cannot violate the law of noncontradiction, but must be consistent within itself.

Matthew 6:24 and Luke 16:13 both say that no one is able to serve two masters:

> *No servant is able to serve two masters, for either he will hate the one and love the other, or he will stand by and be devoted to the one and despise the other. You cannot serve God and*

mammon (riches, or anything in which you trust and on which you rely) (Luke 16:13 AMP).

First Corinthians 10:21 declares, *"You cannot drink the cup of the Lord and the cup of demons too; you cannot have a part in both the Lord's table and the table of demons."*

We must be consistent in the choices we make. If not, we are unstable and can easily be persuaded to change sides in accordance with the circumstances that we are experiencing. James 1:6-7 explains that if we have doubts concerning what we believe, we are double-minded and should not expect to receive anything from the Lord. Joshua put it this way:

If it seems evil to you to serve the Lord, choose for yourselves this day whom you will serve, whether the gods which your fathers served on the other side of the River, or the gods of the Amorites, in whose land you dwell; but as for me and my house, we will serve the Lord (Joshua 24:15 AMP).

There is really no middle ground.

Cohesive

Cohesive means that the system members are working together as a united whole. They are unified, interconnected, solid, organized, and interrelated. Christians are called to become the unified Body of Christ so that:

Then we will no longer be infants, tossed back and forth by the waves, and blown here and there by every wind of teaching and by the cunning and craftiness of men in their deceitful scheming. Instead, speaking the truth in love, we will in all things grow up into Him . . . (Ephesians 4:14-15 NIV).

The Church must cohere so that it presents a formidable argument against the lies of a counterfeit.

Paul urged the Philippians that the way to present a formidable argument against any enemy was to be careful how they conducted themselves in everyday life.

> *Only be sure as citizens* [of the Kingdom] *so to conduct yourselves [that] your manner of life [will be] worthy of the good news (the Gospel) of Christ, so that whether I [do] come and see you or am absent, I may hear this of you: that you are standing firm in united spirit and purpose, striving side by side and contending with a single mind for the faith of the glad tidings (the Gospel)* (Philippians 1:27 AMP).

Peter encouraged the persecuted Christians of Asia Minor that the way to victory was to:

> *...Be of one and the same mind (united in spirit), sympathizing [with one another], loving [each other] as brethren [of one household], compassionate and courteous (tenderhearted and humble)* (1 Peter 3:8 AMP).

Jesus declared, *"Every kingdom divided against itself will be ruined, and every city or household divided against itself will not stand"* (Matt. 12:25 NIV).

Comprehensive

Comprehensive means complete, full, wide-ranging, far-reaching, and thorough. To effectively counter any counterfeit worldview, we must be able to present an answer that gives an explanation to the ultimate purpose and meaning of life. Colossians 1:28 (AMP) says we are to preach and proclaim Jesus in this way:

> *...warning and admonishing everyone and instructing everyone in all wisdom (comprehensive insight into the ways and purposes of God), that we may present every person mature (full-grown, fully initiated, complete, and perfect) in Christ (the Anointed One).*

175

Second Corinthians 10:3-5 tells us that God has called His people to overthrow strongholds and to be able to refute all thoughts, theories, and arguments that come against the knowledge of God. This has to do not only with individual thoughts that become strongholds in a person's mind, but also with thoughts that become the underpinning and presupposition of a whole culture.

For though we walk (live) in the flesh, we are not carrying on our warfare according to the flesh and using mere human weapons. For the weapons of our warfare are not physical [weapons of flesh and blood], but they are mighty before God for the overthrow and destruction of strongholds, [Inasmuch as we] refute arguments and theories and reasonings and every proud and lofty thing that sets itself up against the [true] knowledge of God; and we lead every thought and purpose away captive into the obedience of Christ (the Messiah, the Anointed One) (2 Corinthians 10:3-5 AMP).

We are supposed to mature in our thinking and reasoning so that we can not only defend our Kingdom worldview, but also skillfully teach it and free those who are trapped in the lies of the enemy's counterfeit system.

In summary, the basis of Christianity's belief system, the Bible, fulfills these three C's in the following ways:

Christianity Is Consistent

Although the Bible is composed of 66 different books written over a period of over 1,600 years by about 40 different authors from many different cultural and economic backgrounds who wrote about various subjects—including history, wisdom, psalms, theology, faith, law, and prophecy—the Bible is amazingly harmonious with central themes from Genesis to Revelation that include:

- The Cultural Commission (Genesis 1:28 to Matthew 28:19).

- The Seed of the Woman (Genesis 3:15 to Galatians 3:16-18).

- The Abrahamic Blessing (Genesis 12:1-3 to Galatians 3:29).

- The moral law as found in the Ten Commandments (Exodus 20 to numerous parts of the New Testament that deal with each of these laws; i.e., Exodus 20:12 with Ephesians 6:2-3).

- The Great Commandment as found in Deuteronomy 6:5 and restated and illustrated in Luke 10:25-37. ("The Good Samaritan" story illustrates loving your neighbor, and the Great Commandment is also restated in Matthew 22:37-40.)

- Spiritual Warfare between God (and His people) and the hosts of hell (compare Genesis 3:15, First Chronicles 21:1, Daniel 10:13, and Zechariah 3:1 with Matthew 4:1-11, John 12:31, Ephesians 6:10-19, and Revelation 12:7-13).

Christianity Is Cohesive

The Bible is one unified whole with each part working perfectly together. Although the Bible is harmonious, it has numerous categories, such as The Law, The Prophets, The Psalms, Proverbs, Historical books, Poetical books, The Gospels, The Epistles (which are divided categorically into the church epistles, doctrinal epistles, and pastoral and personal epistles). In addition to this, both the Old and the New Testament perfectly complement each other.

Kevin Conner said in *The Foundations of Christian Doctrine* regarding the harmony between the Old and New Testaments of the Bible:

The New is in the Old contained;

The Old is in the New explained;

The New is in the Old enfolded;

The Old is in the New unfolded,

The New is in the Old concealed,

The Old is in the New revealed."[1]

Christianity Is Comprehensive

The Scriptures present an all-encompassing world and life view that gives us a rational explanation regarding:

- The beginning of all things in Creation (Genesis 1:1 and John 1:1-4).

- The reason for sin, evil, and pain in the world: i.e., the fall of Adam as shown in Genesis 3 caused sin to enter the human race and released hatred and enmity in the world. (Genesis 3:15 shows that the people who are of the Seed of God are at continual odds with the Seed of the serpent. According to Second Corinthians 4:4, satan also became the god of this world and releases evil on the earth in many various forms.)

- The solution for the Fall: Redemption. Through the blood of Jesus the sin of Adam was taken away and now God works all things for good for those who love Him and are called according to His purpose. (Read Romans 5:12-19 and 8:28.)

- The consummation of all things and/or how everything will end. Acts 3:21 and Revelation 21:1-3 show how the end of human life as we know it will culminate when the influence of the Gospel pervades the earth so powerfully that it results in the second bodily return of Jesus Christ to judge the earth.

Other Worldviews and the Three C's

Study and be eager and do your utmost to present yourself to God approved (tested by trial), a workman who has no cause to be ashamed, correctly analyzing and accurately dividing [rightly handling and skillfully teaching] the Word of Truth (2 Timothy 2:15 AMP).

As we go through the following worldview systems that are contrary to our Kingdom worldview, see how you can apply the three

"C's" to each belief system and effectively expose and skillfully refute these counterfeits of the enemy.

In this chapter I have chosen to address three worldviews (Naturalism, the New Age, and Islam), though many others obviously exist. I believe these three are the ones that Christians in the United States are most likely to encounter. It is, however, important to have an understanding of all world belief systems so that you can intelligently refute their beliefs and compare them to the truth of the Bible.[2]

Naturalism

Naturalism is a belief system in which the cosmos is the result of totally natural phenomena without the aid of a supernatural being. This of course contrasts with theism, which espouses the view that the world was created by a God. Belief systems such as atheism, evolutionism, Buddhism, Confucianism, and Taoism would be classified under naturalism. The theistic category would include all of the major religions of the world except Buddhism, which is based on an atheistic system.

The consequences of naturalistic philosophy are huge. When a naturalistic philosophy is the worldview, then the basic assumptions presuppose that there is no supernatural explanation for the creation or ordering of the universe. Thus, there is no transcendent purpose or morality, which leads to a cultural conundrum with no restraint higher than human opinion on behavior. For example, since the Ten Commandments are no longer taught in the public schools, children have no moral compass to live by and are left merely with their natural instincts and personal opinions.

This violates the *consistency* requirement because when personal preference becomes the rule of the day, it creates a cultural cacophony rather than a cultural symphony. We saw the results of this in the fall of 2007 when Venezuelan President Hugo Chavez made numerous economic and political changes, causing cultural chaos and inciting the people of Venezuela to want more government intervention. This then gave him the necessary popular opinion to shore up his political powers, change his nation's constitution, and run for president *ad infinitum*—holding office with no limits to his term.

One of the goals laid out in *The Communist Manifesto* by Karl Marx was to cause a cultural revolution, which would then lead to chaos and prepare the way for communists to come in and save the day, eventually taking over that nation.

As a result of naturalism, various schools of thought have been developed, such as multiculturalism, which attempts to equally respect and adapt itself to different cultures instead of fostering its own overarching culture. In this type of system, there is no transcendent truth, so humans find their primary identity in their ethnic background, gender, and history. Multiculturalism is thus a pluralistic society that can eventually wind up like the Tower of Babel—every person speaks a different language, which hinders them from working together and causes the eventual demise of that nation (see Gen. 11:1-8).

When theistic religions are tolerated in a naturalistic society, like in North America and many nations of Western Europe, the result is a polytheistic society with many gods and multiple religions. Polytheism also leads back to moral relativism, which leads to confusion and chaos and eventually culminates in totalitarianism.

Human nature is such that most people would exchange their freedom of choice and expression for peace and safety. Therefore, if the crime rate ever gets out of control, the people become open to transitioning from a democracy to a dictatorship. We see this happening today as Russian Prime Minister Vladimir Putin consolidates his power more and more by centralizing the control that the Kremlin has over private business, the media, and the country's state governors.

Other branches of naturalism include postmodernism, existentialism, and pragmatism. Postmodernism, as discussed earlier, teaches that truth is relative to a person's opinions, feelings, experiences, and perceptions. Existentialism purports that each individual should create their own meaning and transcendent truth based on how they intuit within. Pragmatism has to do with practicing and legalizing whatever laws work best for the majority of people.

Pragmatism seems to be the hallmark of many of today's conservatives who seem to espouse biblical principles regarding fiscal and social issues, but base their belief system on scientific data rather than solid biblical truths. For example, many conservatives oppose same-sex marriage, not because they believe in the Bible, but because the social data points to traditional marriage as the most important way to have a stable society and raise healthy children. This is why Christians must be careful to not always think that the conservative movement is Christ-centered and that every conservative would welcome God's Kingdom influence on earth.

The highest goal of naturalism is to create some sort of utopia in which the goodness of humanity fully manifests because the cultural elites will rise to power and craft the proper political, economic, and social environment. Naturalism lacks *consistency* because there is no unvarying truth on which to build a solid belief system.

The New Age Movement

The New Age movement *is* a very eclectic term that relates to varying degrees and expressions of Eastern mysticism. Generally speaking, its main belief is that every 2000 years another "Christ" person arises to teach civilization new truth about God and the meaning of life. With every age the revelation gets greater as we all continue to progress toward divinity through greater degrees of enlightenment.

The New Age movement became popular during the cultural revolution of the 1960s when many young people were strongly influenced by contemporary music to rebel against the "plastic" people and values of the 1950s. Their attempts to find a deeper meaning to life led many to turn to Eastern religions that emphasized contentment through harmony with nature and the universe.

Consequently, millions of young people rebelled against the faith of their parents and espoused the Eastern belief that there is divinity in each living thing. They were attracted to the fact that they could become spiritually in touch with themselves and their environment without the "un-cool" restraints of their Judeo-Christian heritage. Although this took place approximately four decades ago, the New Age movement is still prevalent in contemporary culture. The average person seeks for "spirituality" rather than a traditional religion.

Like naturalism, the New Age mindset is *inconsistent* because whatever feels right to the individual becomes truth to him or her. This also prevents a truly cohesive culture because the only central belief is that nothing is absolute truth. Everything is subject to the current circumstances and needs of the moment. This belief system leaves its adherents open to any and all "spirits."

Islam

Islam, which was founded by Mohammed in the sixth century, is formidable because it presents a comprehensive worldview based on the Qur'an. The reason why Hamas (an Islamic terrorist organization) is so powerful in Palestine and recently won the elections and control of the government is because they not only teach religion, but are busy building schools, hospitals, taking care of the poor, and presenting a fully-developed and all-encompassing worldview that is capable of constructing a society and culture under Sharia law.

While the Christians are busy buying the latest books on the last days, Muslims are raising billions of dollars, cutting business deals with the United States and Asia, and developing new oil fields. The conflict with terrorism will not go away anytime soon because Islam has skillfully managed to integrate the propagation of their faith with the world's economy.

Approximately 15 percent of our nation's oil comes from OPEC, whose nations support the global proliferation of Islam and the building of mosques in our neighborhoods. So every time you fill your car with a tank of gas that comes from OPEC, you are inadvertently supporting this Islamic influence.

As I wrote in my previous book:

> While Islam is targeting the cities of America and is possibly the fastest growing urban religion today, more and more Christians are fleeing the cities to pursue a non-threatening life of comfort and ease![3]

Islam appears to be the most formidable counterfeit in our world today since it has created a cohesive culture that can infiltrate and influence not only individuals but also countries. It is, however, *inconsistent* with biblical truth.[4]

Incidentally, our present conflict in the Middle East is really a vivid example of the clash of civilizations between nations influenced by a Christian worldview and those influenced by an Islamic worldview. Because of this competing ideology between these viewpoints, Christians need to fully grasp their own biblical worldview and then apply it by penetrating Middle East cultural systems if they are going to stand a chance at transforming Muslim nations.

Unfortunately, modern Muslims believe and practice the Cultural Mandate presented in Genesis 1:28 more diligently than most Christians. While western Christians often intentionally choose to have smaller families and seem to lack the ability to keep their children in their faith, Muslims are populating the earth with their fully indoctrinated children who are demographically becoming more and more of a majority in Western Europe. They are armed with the goal of taking over Europe and the world for Islam. If Christians do not wake up soon with a fully-developed view of the Kingdom of God, Islam will become the major religious and political force in Europe and many other nations of this earth.

THINK ON THIS

In light of this brief overview of several counterfeit worldviews, Christians need to understand that the only apologia capable of surmounting a sufficient challenge to these counterfeits is a comprehensive, cohesive, and consistent understanding of the Gospel of the Kingdom of God. Christianity provides the only worldview capable of fully comporting with reality and counteracting the enemy's counterfeit worldviews.

We must know the difference between naturalism and theism and what some of the offshoots of naturalism are so as to arm ourselves with the truth of God's Word and not be given over to "hollow philosophies." We should ask ourselves how the New Age movement has been able to manifest itself through various spheres into modern culture and why it is so attractive to our young people. We need to fully understand what makes Islam so effective and why terrorist groups like Hamas have such a strong following in Palestine.

As Christians, we should know that the best way to counter a false worldview is to fully understand the worldview of the Kingdom of God.[5]

Read Second Timothy 2:23-26.

What are some of the ways the apostle Paul instructed Timothy to handle false doctrines and counterfeit teachings?

What are the three "C's" of an effective belief system?

Give an example of each one that substantiates Christianity.

Explain why the three belief systems explained in this chapter do not fulfill these three "C's."

- Naturalism

- The New Age movement

- Islam

Personalize Second Timothy 2:15 as you determine to effectively deal with the influence of the enemy's counterfeit belief systems in our world today.

Endnotes

1. Kevin Conner, *The Foundations of Christian Doctrine* (City Christian Publishing, 2007), 35.

2. For a quick comparison of 11 of the major world religions, see *A Comparison of World Religions* by Henry J. Haydt.

3. Joseph Mattera, *Ruling in the Gates* (Lake Mary, FL: Creation House, 2003), 79.

4. For resources on how to refute Islam, please refer to the following outstanding books: *Answering Islam: The Crescent in Light of the Cross* by Norman Geisler and Abdul Saleeb; *The Quran and the Bible: In the Light of History and Science* by Dr. William Campbell; *The Blood of the Moon: Understanding the Historic Struggle Between Islam and Western Civilization* by George Grant; *Inside Islam: Exposing and Reaching the World of Islam* by Reza F. Safa; and *What Every American Needs to Know About the Qur'an* by William Federer.

5. Read *The Clash of Civilizations and the Remaking of World Order* by Samuel Huntington for a more thorough study of this subject.

CONCLUSION

As the conclusion of this book, my prayer is that those who read this treatise will have a practical and ideological handbook useful for engaging the culture as Salt and Light as instructed in Matthew 5:13-16. My primary theological goal is to shift the starting point of biblical interpretation back to the Cultural Commission of Genesis 1:28 so that unnecessary chatter questioning the validity of the Christian's call to be involved outside the realm of the church can be squelched. My practical goal is to give useful illustrations to pastors, leaders, and future movers and shakers so that they have a model to look to for future cultural engagement. I have attempted to present a balanced approach in this book so that it has an overview of some of the salient theological themes needed to promote and expand God's Kingdom rule in each community of the earth.

Consequently, I have included in these chapters material dealing with the image of God, prayer, Kingdom economics, the power of God, the laws of God, the covenants of God, and an apologetical approach that neatly fits the biblical worldview approach. I am convinced that the expansion and influence of Christianity is the only hope for the future of planet earth before the return of our Lord!

Originally, I had much more material that I was going to include in this book, but my editors suggested that I break up the content into two separate books. My next book will be even more practical and will deal more with leaders partnering together in the Kingdom for the fulfillment of the Cultural Commission as given to us in Genesis 1:28.

On a different note, in the Appendix I have included many examples of how Christianity throughout history has had a significant impact on many different realms of society. Read, be inspired, and be challenged to fulfill your cultural commission to impact this nation for the glory of God.

Before I finish, I want to state that I am well aware of the previous works of others dealing with the subject of the Gospel and societal transformation. One such author, Walter Rauschenbusch (1861-1918), who some consider the premier theologian of the Kingdom of God, expounded a worldview more akin to Marxism. He embraces an economics of equality rather than biblical economics as presented in this book. His series of books include *Christianity and the Social Crisis* (1907), *Christianizing the Social Order* (1912), and *A Theology for the Social Gospel* (1917). He wrote that "social redemption would be marked by the triumph of cooperation over competition, fraternity over coercion and public good over private gain."[1]

Ronald Sider, a contemporary proponent of the utilization of a big central government to aid the poor as shown in his book *Rich Christians in an Age of Hunger,* has already been roundly answered by David Chilton in his book *Prosperous Christians in an Age of Guilt Manipulators.* Jim Wallis, who represents the liberal left wing of evangelical Christianity, wrote a book entitled *God's Politics* that I will briefly critique in my next book on the Kingdom of God.

As we conclude this book, please carefully consider all that has been presented and what the Holy Spirit has stirred up in your spirit concerning Christianity's influence on our world and what God has specifically called you to do.

If you are in a leadership position and would like additional information on how to partner with other Christian leaders to advance God's Kingdom on the earth, read the forthcoming sequel to this book, which will deal with:

- God Ideas, Not Just Good Ideas

- Partnering in the Kingdom

- Partnering and Ethnicity

- Partnering for Corporate Destiny

- Partnering Within the Apostolic Reformation

- Partnering for the Progress of the Kingdom

- Partnering Under the Law of the Kingdom

- The Five Models of the Kingdom

- The Power of Synergism

See the contact information at the end of this book for details on how to keep abreast regarding the purchase of Part 2 of this work when it comes out in the near future.

Endnote

1. Walter Rauschenbusch, quoted in Adrian Hastings, ed., *A World History of Christianity* (Grand Rapids, MI: Wm. B. Eerdmans Publishing Company, 2000), 443.

APPENDIX

CHRISTIANITY'S IMPACT IN CULTURE

The works of the Lord are great, sought out of all them that have pleasure therein (Psalm 111:2).

Science

While it is popular today to speak about keeping religion out of science, most do not know that it was Christianity that paved the way for science. Some of science's greatest contributors claimed to be followers of Christ. Famous and influential scientists like William of Occam (1285-1347), Leonardo da Vinci (1452-1519), Galileo (1564-1642), Blaise Pascal (1623-1662), Roger Bacon (1214-1294), Nicholas Copernicus (1473-1543), Johannes Kepler (1571-1630), Isaac Newton (1642-1727), Louis Pasteur (1822-1895), George Washington Carver (1864-1943), and other major scientists not included in this list made major discoveries regarding scientific methodology, experimentation, empirical observation, astronomy, mathematics, the laws of gravity, health care, medical treatment, agriculture, and more. The names and their contributions are too numerous to mention here.

Until the 19th century, science was known as a natural philosophy and was considered a branch of divinity, the queen of the sciences. Christian theism provided the impetus for such study. The rationale was that if there was a personal God who designed everything that exists with rational natural laws, then it would be possible to discover those laws through careful study.

Those with a naturalistic worldview have no real impetus for such study given their impersonal and random starting point and their views of the evolutionary process of the cosmos. After all, if life is merely matter in motion plus time and chance, how could we discover any unifying principles useful for empirical laboratory experimentation?

Natural science has to presuppose Christian theism because, for example, the naturalistic worldview on its own cannot assume the ability to predict the future based on observing the past. An impersonal random process doesn't allow for predictability. Since Christianity presupposes a designer who had a purpose in creation, it is easy to believe in set patterns and/or laws in nature that ensure predictability. Without a creator for the universe, we are left only with randomness—which then abrogates the natural law trajectory that science presently uses to calculate future results.

Because the universe has a creator, we can safely say that there is design and set laws. These set laws, for example, enable a scientist who wants to create water to use the formula of combining the properties of hydrogen and oxygen. With the proper mix (H_2O) and the correct environment, a scientist can always expect to produce water. If, on the other hand, the universe has no design and came about by a chance interaction of matter and motion, there would be no rational foundation to believe that we can deliberately discover any set laws in the universe that would enable us to create water or any other properties.

Another simple illustration is the Law of Gravity. We understand by studying the gravitational pull on the earth that objects have weight based on their mass. Because of this, when a person jumps up (while on earth), they can expect to come back down at a speed determined by a combination of several measurable factors (e.g., their weight and inches off the ground). If, on the other hand, there was no cosmological designer, then gravity would be as unpredictable as a piece of dust blowing in the wind. The way a person comes back down to the ground after jumping would always be a unique event in which sometimes they may go up and not come down or sometimes they may go sideways. Only Christianity has the necessary *Weltanschauung* (German word for "worldview") to provide a rational basis for scientific study.

Music

From King David and the Book of Psalms to the hymns sung by Jesus and the apostles in the upper room at the last supper, music has been an influential part of the Christian faith. Music has not stayed within the confines of the Church, but has greatly affected all cultures. Prior to the tenth century, most singing was atonal or inharmonious. The Church introduced harmony in music, which paved the way for some of the greatest music the world has ever known.

World musical geniuses such as Johann Sebastian Bach (1685–1750), George Frederic Handel (1685–1759), Ludwig van Beethoven (1770–1827), Felix Mendelssohn (1809–47), and Johannes Brahms (1833–97), were all influenced by Christianity and largely wrote music for the glory of God.

The fact that a believer in Christ brought about the breakthrough with tonal music is logical if you take into account the Christian belief that God created the cosmos with a design and a purpose (see Eph. 1:10; Rev. 4:11). Thus it is a *uni*verse made up of complex yet unified and harmonious systems. This logically leads to the discovery of acute harmony in all aspects of the created order.

This is in contrast to a "*multi*verse" made up of a purposeless matter in motion that unexplainably leads to what appears to be a design, but really is not. The "sound" produced without harmony, order, and unity would resemble the chaotic "noise" of an orchestra warming up prior to a concert.

Philosophy and Literature

Since Christianity is a consistent, comprehensive, and cohesive worldview, its adherents have been involved with preaching and demonstrating the Gospel of the Kingdom, which includes the production of philosophical writings and literature that have greatly impacted Western civilization.

Perhaps the best example of this is *The City of God* by St. Augustine (fourth century A.D.). It has been perhaps the most influential book in history, with the exception of the Bible. Its philosophy of history became the impetus for many world-changers including King Charlemagne, Pope Nicholas I, Pope Gregory VII, John Calvin, and Abraham Kuyper, all of whom endeavored to establish the Kingdom of God on earth by applying the principles of Christianity not only to the church, but also to political, judicial, educational, industrial, and cultural spheres.

Another influential book was the *Summa Theologica* by St. Thomas Aquinas. His ideas regarding natural law and how the human mind can receive truth apart from divine revelation forever affected the landscape of human history and eventually led to Francis Bacon's empirical methodology for science that is still in use today. Because Aquinas taught that there is truth in human reason outside of direct revelation of the Scriptures or the Holy Spirit, it opened up a door in society in which truth was then separated from divine revelation. This motivated people to do experiments, utilizing their power of reason and the human senses of sight, smell, hearing, and touch in empirical experimentation.

Also of note is *The Institutes of the Christian Religion* by John Calvin (16th century), which not only provided the Church with the most comprehensive systematic approach to theology in its history, but also influenced the way Western Europe and the future United States viewed the relationship between church and state, the proper role of civil magistrates, and most importantly, the sovereignty of God. The latter view aided theologians for centuries to come (most notably Abraham Kuyper) because it further illustrated how believers should have a fully-developed, well-rounded biblical world and life views. It correlates God's sovereign involvement with His created order inside and outside the Church.

The Pilgrim's Progress by John Bunyan (1628–88) was so popular that it became one of the books of choice to help educate school children. Some of its phraseology and language seeped into the English language and affected the morals of Europe and America.

Also of note is *Paradise Lost,* the great epic poem by the blind poet John Milton (1608–74), which is one of the books selected for the Great Books of the Western World collection. Milton's work dominated English poetry in the 18th and 19th centuries and its popularity in scholarly and literary circles (both secular and Christian) continues to the present day. The powerful impact on society and culture that *Paradise Lost* had is evidenced in our modern-day English language. Most people are unaware that many of the words they use every day were first coined in Milton's work—*jubilant, dreary, satanic, acclaim, unaided, impassive, enslaved, pandemonium, rebuff, self-esteem* and hundreds of others!

Pensees by Blaise Pascal (1623–62) is an unfinished apologia for the Christian religion upon which Pascal's reputation now rests. The *Pensees* is a collection of philosophical fragments, notes, and essays in which Pascal explores the contradictions of human nature in psychological, social, metaphysical, and, above all, theological terms. Mankind emerges from Pascal's analysis as a wretched and desolate creature within an impersonal universe, but also as a being whose existence can be transformed through faith in God's grace.

A Christmas Carol by Charles Dickens (1812–70) is still one of the most popular Christmas stories and is depicted in numerous plays and television shows two centuries after it was penned. It shows the transforming power of an extra-worldly encounter, the visitation of three spirits, that confronted Scrooge with the sinfulness of his self-centeredness and greed causing him to repent from his evil ways. It has been used for well over 100 years to depict the possibility of transformation through repentance.

Uncle Tom's Cabin by Harriet Beecher Stowe (1811–96), an anti-slavery novel, became one of the favorite books of the abolitionist movement. The name of one of its principle characters, Uncle Tom, is still used as a pejorative to depict a black person "selling out" his own people to the oppressive white social construct in order to ensure self-preservation. So great was the influence of this book that historians credited it with intensifying the sectional conflicts that led to the Civil War.

The Protestant Ethic and the Spirit of Capitalism by Max Weber (1864–1920) was a groundbreaking book that displays the correlation between hard work, capitalism, and the influence of the Protestant Reformation. *The Protestant Ethic* therefore gave a religious impetus for rigorous discipline that encouraged men to apply themselves rationally to acquire wealth.

Finally, *Mere Christianity,* penned by noted Christian Oxford professor C.S. Lewis (1898–1963) was one of the most rational presentations of the basics of Christianity ever presented and has been used to bring the Gospel to millions of people. Many consider this the most influential Christian book of the 20th century.

Of course, no list would be complete without mentioning the immense influence the King James Version of the Bible has had on English literature and its language in particular—the language of choice for the developing world for more than a century. All one has to do is read the writings of Shakespeare for a salient example of this point. Whole books have been devoted to the subject of the King James Version Bible and its influence, but suffice it to say that Christianity and the Scriptures have forever altered every aspect of life and culture.[1]

Words and Symbols

The words and symbols introduced by the Church illustrate the enormous influence that the Kingdom of God has had on the English language. Words are vital to the formation and structure of a culture. If you want to change a culture, you must first create a new vocabulary or redefine its key words and phrases.

For example, our present culture first changed the way we described certain biblically immoral practices before the culture could be desensitized to the sin and transition to a post-Christian, postmodern ethos. Words like *homosexual* have been replaced with *gay* (read a novel from the early 1970s or earlier and you will see that *gay* previously meant "happy"). The biblical term to describe an immoral woman who sells sex (*whore*) has been replaced with *ladies of the night.* The word *adultery* has been replaced with the word *affair,* and so forth.

The following are words and symbols that are still in use but that were introduced by the Church into the mainstream culture hundreds of years ago:

1. A.D.: *Anno Domini,* in the year of our Lord after His birth.

2. B.C.: Before the birth of Christ.

3. Cathedral: Church of a bishop's seat.

4. Cemetery: For Christians, a temporary sleeping place for the dead.

5. Chapel: Secondary sanctuary for Christian worship.

6. Christmas tree: Signifies Christ's birth as the tree of life.

7. Church: Building for divine services and synonymous with Christianity.

8. Creed: A formal statement of beliefs, especially Christian doctrine.

9. Cross: Symbol of Christ's death and identity symbol of Christians.

10. Heaven: The eternal abode of God, the angels, and saved believers.

11. Hell: The eternal abode of the devil, his angels, and lost humanity.

12. Heresy: A teaching that denies basic Christian beliefs.

13. Martyr: A Christian witness who dies for his faith.

14. Pagan: A non-Christian.

15. Parish: A geographic area of church members.

16. Pastor: The spiritual head of a group of Christians.

17. Trinity: God as Father, Son, and Holy Spirit.[2]

Expressions and Sayings

The following expressions and sayings have also become part of the English language and illustrate how Christianity and the Scriptures have permeated every aspect of culture.

- "Good Samaritan" — refers to Jesus' parable in Luke 10:30-37.

- "Avoid it like the plague" — is from St. Jerome in the early fifth century.

- "Brother" — a concept expressed by Jesus in Matthew 5:21-24.

- "Doubting Thomas" — Thomas doubting Christ's resurrection.

- "Filthy lucre" — St. Paul in Titus 1:11.

- "Harmless as doves" — Matthew 10:16.

- "Thorn in the flesh" — Second Corinthians 12:7.

- "Rob Peter to pay Paul" — refers to Saints Peter and Paul.

- "Turn the other cheek" — Jesus' Sermon on the Mount in Matthew Chapter 5.

- "When in Rome, do as the Romans do" — St. Ambrose in the fourth century.

- "Wolf in sheep's clothing" — Matthew 7:15.[3]

Laws and Principles

The Ten Commandments and the application of Mosaic civic law to culture have been the moral and economic underpinnings for many a nation, social contract, and national constitution. The following laws and principles came from the Bible:

1. Laws regarding capital gains. Luke 19:13-26 and Matthew 25:14-29 demonstrate how a person can expand his finances exponentially by investing it where it appreciates.

2. Laws and/or principles against progressive income tax (see Lev. 27:32; 1 Sam. 8:14-15).

3. Laws regarding estate tax and leaving an inheritance are referred to in Proverbs 13:22.

4. Laws regarding minimum wage are discussed in Matthew 20:1-15.

5. Laws regarding local, state, county, and federal officials are expounded on in Exodus 18:21. In principle, Moses set up a system of representative government over Israel, from a local to a national level, with leaders who would judge Israel by overseeing as little as ten people and on up to thousands of citizens.

6. Laws for setting up judges to adjudicate between citizens are explained in Deuteronomy 16:18-20 and in Second Chronicles 19:4-7.

7. Laws that the national leader cannot be foreign born are expressed in Deuteronomy 17:15.

8. Laws that credible witnesses must verify a judgment against someone are found in Deuteronomy 17:6 and Exodus 23:1.

9. Laws regarding cleanliness to stop the spread of disease are explained in Deuteronomy 23:10-14 and in Leviticus 12:1-4; 13; 15:2-13. Those regarding health inspections in homes are found in Leviticus 14:33-40.

10. Laws against kidnapping are listed in Deuteronomy 24:7 and in Exodus 21:16.

11. Laws regarding devaluing monetary currency are listed in Deuteronomy 25:13-15.

12. Laws against bribery that perverts justice are found in Exodus 23:6-8.

13. Laws regarding murder are expounded upon in Exodus 21:12.

14. Laws regarding injury or death to an unborn child are clearly explained in Exodus 21:22-24.

15. Laws regarding monetary compensation for loss of employment due to accident or injury are seen in Exodus 21:18-19.

16. Laws regarding not returning runaway slaves are found in Deuteronomy 23:15-16.

17. Laws regarding rape and incest are explained in Leviticus 18:6-10 and Deuteronomy 22:25-27.

18. Laws regarding self-defense against burglary are found in Exodus 22:2-3.

19. Laws against mob violence and rioting are dealt with in Exodus 23:2.

20. Laws regarding immigration and citizenship are explained in Deuteronomy 10:9; 27:19; Ezekiel 47:21-22; Jeremiah 7:5-7; and Leviticus 19:34.

21. Laws regarding charitable loans are covered in Exodus 22:25 and Leviticus 25:35-37.

22. Laws regarding the length of loans are explained in Deuteronomy 15:12.

23. Laws regarding exemption from serving in the army are found in Deuteronomy 20:5-8.

24. Laws against excessive punishment for a crime are explained in Deuteronomy 25:3.

The United States Government

Christian evangelist George Whitfield has been called the Father of the American Revolution because his preaching helped unite the 13 colonies during the first Great Awakening. So many ministers were involved in the war—using the pulpit to gain support for independence—that the British called our actions "The Parson's Rebellion" or the "Black Robe Rebellion."

The Christian influence on our nation is without question. For nearly two centuries, Americans started legislative sessions by bringing in preachers to tell the Senate and the House of Representatives what the Word of God said about civil government.

As I write this, there are 29 nations currently involved in a revolution. The period during the American Revolution was called the Age of Revolutions. Since the birth of our nation, France has had 15 different governments. Poland has had seven just since 1991, and Italy is working on their 54th. The stability that the American civil system has had for the past 233 years, in comparison to these other nations, makes it seem obvious that God has greatly blessed the Christian influence on our nation's founding!

Regarding the signers of the Declaration of Independence, we have all been trained to recognize the least religious men who signed the Declaration: George Washington and James Madison. But 24 of them were seminarians. Thomas Jefferson was one of the only slave owners among the signers. Seventy percent of the signers were abolitionists. Where did they get their ideas? They got them from John Locke's *Two Treatises of Government*. It quotes the Bible over 1,700 times and is the basis of the Declaration of Independence.

Locke was also sourced for the Constitution. One example of the biblical influence on our Constitution is found in the Executive branch. Deuteronomy 17:15 says that the top national leader for Israel had to be born in Israel. The U.S. Constitution also forbids a foreign-born person from becoming president. Also, laws regarding the judiciary influenced the formation of the U.S. Supreme Court (see Deut. 16:18-20), and laws regarding the eldership of Israel (see Exod. 18:19-23) served as the template for the Congress of the United States. James Madison, an author of the Constitution of the United States, said this:

We have staked the whole future of our new nation, not upon the power of government; far from it. We have staked the future of all our political constitutions upon the capacity of each of ourselves to govern ourselves according to the moral principles of the Ten Commandments.

Marriage and Family

Christianity brought western civilization back to the original template for marriage found in Genesis 2 (God placed one man with one woman). Because of the Fall, God allowed divorce and polygamy in the Old Covenant. But after the incarnation of Christ and the power of the Holy Spirit came to all believers, the standard for marriage was once again raised.

In the New Testament, a person couldn't be a leader in a congregation unless he was the husband of only one wife as explained in First Timothy 3:2,12 and Titus 1:6. In addition, in Matthew 5:32 and again in Matthew 19:9, Jesus taught that you cannot legally divorce your spouse unless your spouse is found to be an adulterer.

These standards became the standard for western civilization for the past 2,000 years. But they are presently under attack by the proponents of alternate forms of marriage, such as same-sex marriage.

Compassion Ministries to the Poor

Since its inception, the Church has been involved in compassionate and charitable ministry to the poor and vulnerable members of society. Biblical passages such as Luke 10:30-37, which tells about the Good Samaritan, and Matthew 25:35-36, which teaches about Judgment Day, have had a profound effect on how the world has viewed charity. First Timothy 5:3-16 shows how the early Church supported widows who had been faithful servants of the Church.

Regarding Greco-Roman treatment of the sick, historian Alvin Schmidt says:

Human compassion, especially with regard to the sick and dying, among the ancients was rare, notably among the Greco-Romans. As with the practice of charity, such behavior was contrary to their cultural ethos and to the teachings of the pagan philosophers. For instance, Plato (427–347 B.C.) said that a poor man (usually a slave) who was no longer able to work because of sickness should be left to die. The Roman philosopher Plautus (254–184 B.C.) argued, "You do a beggar bad service by giving him food and drink; you lose what you give and prolong his life for more misery."

As early as the fourth century, Basil of Caesarea and St. Chrysostom urged the construction of orphanages. Christians also showed their concern for potential orphans by requiring a godly couple to stand with the parents at a child's baptism so that in case the parents died there would be replacements to raise the child.

In more recent history we have seen how the Church has led the way in compassion ministries. America has always been a shining example of charity, beginning with the Pilgrims, who took care of those who were stricken with sicknesses. Alexis de Tocqueville visited the United States in 1831 and credited the influence of the nation's churches to the habit of volunteerism and charity in America.

Numerous voluntary associations have sprung up to provide humanitarian aid to the poor; among the most prominent are the Kiwanis Club, Lion's Club, and Rotary Club. These clubs and others were widely influenced by the Christian ethos of giving that exists in this country.

In England, the YMCA started to help young men who came to London from rural areas to find work. Their original objective was "the winning of young men to Jesus Christ, and the building in them of Christian character."

Child labor laws were reformed in England by Parliamentarian Lord Shaftesbury (1801–85). Spurred on by his intense Christian faith, he single-handedly reformed the laws until England banned all child labor in factories and mines.

The Salvation Army originated in England as a Christian mission founded in 1860 by William and Catherine Booth. Their effect was so great that when they came to America the movement spread rapidly. They not only preached the salvation message, but ministered holistically to all the physical needs of a person. Among other things, they established a "poor man's bank," day care centers, free legal aid, and ministry to prostitutes. Their work for the poor spurred on progressive reforms and provided the impetus for new legislation.

Most recently, Christian organizations like World Vision and the Salvation Army have received acclaim for their relief work after catastrophic events like the 9/11 terrorist attacks in New York City, the tsunami in Indonesia, various earthquakes in other nations, and Hurricane Katrina in the United States.

Clearly, biblical teachings and Christian morals have had an incredible impact throughout history. We are wise to remember how much we have benefitted, as a culture and as a nation, from the Word of God; and we must fight to revive the waning Christian influence in our culture today.

Endnotes

1. Read *In the Beginning* by Alister McGrath for more on the impact that the KJV has had on western civilization.

2. Alvin J. Schmidt, *Under the Influence: How Christianity Transformed Civilization* (Grand Rapids, MI: Zondervan Publishing House, 2001), 390-400.

3. *Ibid.*

Author Ministry Page

www.JosephMattera.org

Other Book by Joseph Mattera

Ruling in the Gates
(Lake Mary, FL: Creation House, 2003)

Additional copies of this book and other
book titles from DESTINY IMAGE are
available at your local bookstore.

Call toll-free: 1-800-722-6774.

Send a request for a catalog to:

Destiny Image₀ Publishers, Inc.

P.O. Box 310
Shippensburg, PA 17257-0310

*"Speaking to the Purposes of God for This
Generation and for the Generations to Come."*

For a complete list of our titles,
visit us at www.destinyimage.com.